2014 中国国际旅游研讨会文集

COLLECTED WORKS
OF CHINA INTERNATIONAL TOURISM FORUM
2014

中国旅游研究院
China Tourism Academy

国家旅游局旅游促进与国际合作司
Tourism Promotion and International Cooperation Department of China National Tourism Administration

 编

北京·旅游教育出版社

特约编辑：李　薇
责任编辑：郭珍宏

图书在版编目（CIP）数据

2014中国国际旅游研讨会文集 / 中国旅游研究院，国家旅游局旅游促进与国际合作司主编． -- 北京 ：旅游教育出版社，2017.11

ISBN 978-7-5637-3668-3

Ⅰ．①2… Ⅱ．①中… ②国… Ⅲ．①国际旅游—旅游业发展—中国—文集 Ⅳ．①F592.3-53

中国版本图书馆CIP数据核字(2017)第289416号

2014中国国际旅游研讨会文集

中国旅游研究院
国家旅游局旅游促进与国际合作司　主编

出版单位	旅游教育出版社
地　　址	北京市朝阳区定福庄南里1号
邮　　编	100024
发行电话	（010）65778403　65728372　65767462（传真）
本社网址	www.tepcb.com
E - mail	tepfx@163.com
排版单位	北京旅教文化传播有限公司
印刷单位	北京中科印刷有限公司
经销单位	新华书店
开　　本	787毫米×1092毫米　1/16
印　　张	13
字　　数	142千字
版　　次	2017年11月第1版
印　　次	2017年11月第1次印刷
定　　价	200.00元（海外发行 USD 150）

（图书如有装订差错请与发行部联系）

《2014中国国际旅游研讨会文集》编委会

主任委员　杜　江　国家旅游局副局长　教授　博士

编　　委　戴　斌　中国旅游研究院院长　教授　博士
　　　　　刘士军　国家旅游局旅游促进与国际合作司司长
　　　　　张西龙　国家旅游局旅游促进与国际合作司副司长
　　　　　封立涛　国家旅游局旅游促进与国际合作司副司长

《2014中国国际旅游研讨会文集》编辑部

主　　编　戴　斌　中国旅游研究院院长　教授　博士

执行主编　蒋依依　中国旅游研究院国际旅游研究所所长　副研究员　博士
　　　　　李创新　中国旅游研究院国际旅游研究所博士

成　　员　杨劲松　杨丽琼　宋慧林　张　敏　童时萍　蔡文婧
　　　　　陈小姣　晏　梅　宋丽娜

Editorial Board of Collected Works of China International Tourism Forum 2014

Chairman Prof. and Dr. Du Jiang, Vice Chairman of China National Tourism Administration

Board Member Prof. and Dr. DAI Bin, President of China Tourism Academy

LIU Shijun, Director-General of Tourism Promotion and International Cooperation Department of China National Tourism Administration

ZHANG Xilong, Deputy Director-General of Tourism Promotion and International Cooperation Department of China National Tourism Administration

FENG Litao, Deputy Director-General of Tourism Promotion and International Cooperation Department of China National Tourism Administration

Editorial Department of Collected Works of China International Tourism Forum 2014

Chief Editor Prof. and Dr. DAI Bin, President of China Tourism Academy

Executive Editor Dr. and Associate Professor JIANG Yiyi, Director of Institute of International Tourism Development of China Tourism Academy

Dr. LI Chuangxin, Institute of International Tourism Development of China Tourism Academy

Member YANG Jinsong, YANG Liqiong, SONG Huilin, ZHANG Min, TONG Shiping, CAI Wenjing, CHEN Xiaojiao, YAN Mei, SONG Lina

目 录
CONTENTS

上篇　致辞与总结

在2014中国国际旅游研讨会开幕式上的致辞（1）……………李金早　2

在2014中国国际旅游研讨会开幕式上的致辞（2）………塔勒布·瑞法依　5

在2014中国国际旅游研讨会闭幕式上的总结发言（1）…………杜　江　8

在2014中国国际旅游研讨会闭幕式上的总结发言（2）…………祝善忠　10

中篇　主旨演讲　中国国际旅游的机遇与挑战

美丽中国旅游梦………………………………………………………戴　斌　14

世界旅游的发展趋势…………………………………………………徐　京　19

中国旅游的品牌传播…………………………………………………何海明　22

中国游客消费行为分析………………………………………………董　力　26

下篇　发言与讨论

主题演讲一　入境旅游：如何促进中国入境旅游的持续增长………杨卫武　32

互联网时代的媒体营销——杭州旅游营销的经典案例分享…………李　虹　33

散客化时代的市场开发与产品创新…………………………………于宁宁　41

BBC 关于中国入境旅游报告 ……………………………………… 徐　倩　44

主题研讨一　中国入境旅游的持续增长与推广建议 ……………… 杨卫武　48

中国入境旅游市场持续发展的推广方案 …………………………… 邹新强　50

增进 VISA 刷卡消费，提升中国入境旅游市场的质量 ……… 罗斯·杰克逊　52

德国游客对中国的认知变化与散客化趋势下的游客新诉求 … 马库斯·瓦尔特　54

印度游客的偏好特征与当前赴华旅游的障碍因素 ………… 维卡斯·坎杜利　56

主题演讲二　出境旅游：如何分享中国出境旅游的发展机遇 ……… 徐　京　59

中国出境游客满意度报告 …………………………………………… 李仲广　60

中国出境旅游分析——市场结构和趋势 …………………………… 王新军　64

非洲与中东开门迎接中国游客 ……………………………… 阿姆尔·加法尔　67

中国与中东欧旅游合作 ……………………………………… 阿达姆·如辛科　70

南太平洋岛屿——下一个旅游目的地 ……………………… 索利亚·亨特　74

主题研讨二　转型中的中国出境旅游——机遇、潜力及挑战 ……… 王新军　77

中国出境旅游市场的新变化与新特征 ……………………………… 张士刚　78

以更优质的航空服务应对中国出境旅游的市场转型 ……………… 何志刚　80

新西兰旅游产品的更新与面向中国游客的优质服务 ……… 大卫·克雷格　82

中国出境旅游市场的特征与意大利的努力方向 …………… 里卡尔多·斯特拉诺　84

东盟吸引中国出境旅游市场的巨大潜力与面临挑战 ……………… 吴大伟　86

独具特色的埃及欢迎中国出境游客到访 …………………………… 阿　布　88

Session 1　Opening Remark & Closing Speech

Opening Remark on China International Tourism Forum 2014 (1) … Mr. LI Jinzao　90

Opening Remark on China International Tourism Forum 2014 (2) … Dr. Taleb Rifai　94

Closing Speech on China International Tourism Forum 2014 (1) …… Mr. DU Jiang　98

Closing Speech on China International
　　Tourism Forum 2014 (2) ……………………………… Mr. ZHU Shanzhong　100

Session 2 Keynote Speech
Opportunities and Challenges of China's International Tourism

Beautiful China, Tourism Dream .... Mr. DAI Bin 104

World Tourism Trend .... Mr. XU Jing 112

Brand Promotion of China's Tourism .... Mr. HE Haiming 116

Analysis on the Consumption Behavior of Chinese Tourists .... Mr. DONG Li 122

Session 3 Panel Discussion

Panel Speech 1 China's Inbound Tourism Session: How to Promote
    Sustainable Growth of China's Inbound Tourism .. Prof. YANG Weiwu 128

Media Marketing in the Internet Era .... Mr. Li Hong 129

Development and Innovation of Tourism Products in the FIT Era ... Ms. Yu Ningning 139

BBC's Report On China's Inbound Tourism .... Ms. Katy Xu 144

Panel Discussion 1 Discussion on How to Maintain Sustainable Growth of China's
    Inbound Tourism and the Promotion .... Prof. YANG Weiwu 149

Marketing Plan for Sustainable Development of China's Inbound
    Tourism .... Mr. Tsou Hsin Chiang 151

Quality Improvement of China's Inbound Tourism Market by Promoting Consumption of
    VISA Card .... Mr. Ross Jackson 153

Changes of German Tourists' Demands in FIT Era .... Mr. Markus Walter 155

Preferences of Indian Tourists and Barriers of India-China Tourism
    Market .... Mr. Vikas Khanduri 157

Panel Speech 2 China's Outbound Tourism Session: How to Share the
    Opportunity of China's Outbound Tourism .... Mr. XU Jing 160

2013 Chinese Outbound Tourist Satisfaction Investigation
    Report .... Dr. LI Zhongguang 161

China's Outbound Tourism Analysis—Market Structure and
  Trend ………………………………………… Mr. WANG Xinjun 167
The Middle East and North Africa Open the Door for Chinese
  Tourists ……………………………………… Mr. Amr Ghaffar 171
The Tourism Cooperation between China and Central/Eastern
  Europe ……………………………………… Mr. Adam Ruszinka 175
South Pacific Islands—The Next Destinations …………… Ms. Sonja Hunter 180
Panel Discussion 2   China Outbound Tourism in Transformation-Opportunities,
  Potential and Challenges ………………………… Mr. WANG Xinjun 183
Emerging Changes and Characteristics of China Outbound Tourism
  Market ……………………………………… Mr. ZHANG Shigang 185
Adapting to the Transformation of China Outbound Tourism Market with Better Airline
  Services ……………………………………… Mr. HE Zhigang 188
Upgrading of New Zealand Tourist Products & Quality Service to Chinese
  Tourists ……………………………………… Mr. David Craig 191
Characteristics of China Outbound Tourism Market & Italian
  Interpretation ……………………………… Mr. Riccardo Strano 193
Huge Potential & Challenges ASEAN Attracting Chinese
  Tourists ……………………………………… Mr. WU Dawei 195
Egyptian Unique Tourist Products & Tailor-Made Services to Attract Chinese Outbound
  Tourists …………………………………… Dr. Abualmaaty Shaarawy 197

上篇
致辞与总结

在2014中国国际旅游研讨会开幕式上的致辞（1）

李金早

中国国家旅游局局长

（2014年11月14日，中国 上海）

尊敬的塔勒布·瑞法依秘书长，

克罗地亚旅游部部长达尔科·洛伦钦先生，

牙买加旅游和休闲部部长威克姆·麦克尼尔先生，

苏丹旅游、古迹与野生动物部部长穆罕默德·阿卜杜勒·卡里姆·胡德先生，

俄罗斯联邦旅游署代理署长萨夫诺夫先生，

捷克地方发展部第一副部长克莱拉·多斯塔洛娃女士，

匈牙利经济部旅游事务国务秘书阿达姆·如辛科先生，

葡萄牙经济部旅游国务秘书阿道弗·努内斯先生，

立陶宛经济部副部长阿萨·梅德杰雷，

老挝新闻文化和旅游部副部长蔡达榆先生，

库克群岛旅游部副部长泰珠·罗曼先生，

斐济工业部和旅游部副部长罗拉·安尼·艾迪先生，

萨摩亚旅游局局长索利亚·亨特女士，

津巴布韦旅游部常秘麦凯隆，

美国商务部旅游旅行办公室执行主任凯利·克莱格海德女士，

美国内华达州副州长格雷·肯尼迪先生。

女士们、先生们：

大家好！值此2014中国国际旅游交易会开幕之际，中国国家旅游局和联合国世界旅游组织在这里共同举办中国国际旅游研讨会。在这里，我代表中国国家旅游局对出席研讨会的各位嘉宾表示热烈欢迎！对长期以来一直关心和支持中国旅游业发展的联合国世界旅游组织和瑞法依秘书长以及来自各个国家的朋友们表示衷心的感谢！

我们今天研讨会的主题是"体验美丽中国、共享发展机遇"，这正是为了顺应不断发展变化的世界，以新的视角思考和拓展旅游合作，充分挖掘旅游业的巨大潜力。在此我想提几点建议。

一、共同探讨旅游业发展特别是扩大旅游市场对经济社会发展的重要拉动作用

当前，世界经济正在缓慢复苏。旅游作为世界第一大产业，其引擎作用大有可言。2013年旅游业增加值占全球GDP的近10%，对全球经济增长的贡献达3.1%，创造了1亿多个直接就业岗位。作为世界旅游业的重要组成，中国旅游业在中国政府的正确领导下，伴随着改革开放，实现了跨越式发展。旅游已成为人民生活水平提高的一个重要指标，旅游业正成为国民经济的战略性支柱产业。中国国家主席习近平阁下指出：旅游是综合性产业，是拉动经济发展的重要动力。中国国务院总理李克强强调：加快旅游业改革发展，是适应人民群众消费升级和产业结构调整的必然要求。这些重要的判断是符合实际的。据测算，旅游对餐饮零售业的贡献率超过40%，对文化娱乐业的贡献超过50%，对民航铁路客运业的贡献超过80%，对住宿业的贡献超过90%，商务、留学等活动都以旅游这一综合性产业为载体。此外，各国发展旅游业和拓展入境、出境旅游市场的阶段、道路、经验不尽相同，旅游市场在各自旅游产业中的地位、对经济社会的贡献也不尽相同，我们要在此次研讨会上对这些特点进行讨论。

二、深入探讨旅游业发展特别是扩大旅游市场对国家关系的作用

我们要探讨旅游业发展对改善、加强民间交往、交流所发挥的作用。国与国的关系，归根到底是人与人的关系。正所谓"国之交在于民相亲，民相亲在于民相往"。没有交流，则很多原本正常的事情都会成为误解、隔阂甚至冲突。因此，旅游业的发展对于世界的和平、邻国之间的和平以及人类共同理想、共同愿景的实现，都能起到良好的载体作用。

三、共同探讨旅游业发展特别是旅游市场运行的基本规律及新形势下扩大旅游市场的措施和办法

各个国家都在发展，但是各个国家的具体情况皆不相同，因此我们要就如何管理旅游市场、如何开放旅游资源、如何在保护的前提下用好旅游资源等问题进行共同探讨，交流各自的经验。此次会议的参与者包括来自很多国家的旅游领军人物，你们对旅游业的发展都很有心得，希望大家能够借此机会分享各自经验，促使世界旅游业进步不断提升到新的水平。

四、探讨旅游领域的国际合作

与其他领域相比，旅游业的合作应该是最没有障碍、最能够引起大家共识的。如何利用旅游业的这一特点来加强合作？我们需要就此进行共同探讨。我们有一些经济、贸易领域的区域和次区域合作机制，但在旅游领域此种机制相对缺乏。在这里，我们呼吁建立更多、更加灵活的，能够为广大旅游者和旅游景区所在地带来更大实惠的旅游运作机制。为此，我们要彼此交流，做些细谈。

最后，我祝愿此次研讨会圆满成功！我也再一次代表中国国家旅游局对瑞法依秘书长、联合国世界旅游组织官员长期以来给予的支持表示感谢！对各国旅游主管部门负责人和旅游企业代表莅临中国上海表示欢迎！谢谢大家！

在2014中国国际旅游研讨会开幕式上的致辞（2）

塔勒布·瑞法依

联合国世界旅游组织秘书长

（2014年11月14日，中国 上海）

尊敬的中国国家旅游局局长李金早先生，

再次祝贺此次论坛的顺利召开！我们已经有一个很好的开始，在这个意义非凡的上午，我们承诺定会全力支持您、支持中国、支持亚洲、支持全世界的旅游事业！

尊敬的中国国家旅游局副局长杜江先生，

女士们、先生们，

朋友们：

我很荣幸受邀出席此次研讨会。首先，我想先跟大家说，"你好""早上好"（译注：此处发言人用中文问好）。也特别感谢中国国家旅游局。贵局一直以来都是我们亲密的合作伙伴，此次的合作便是很好的例子。这是联合国世界旅游组织首次出席研讨会的开幕式，此次研讨会意义重大，我们将积极建言献策。

2014中国国际旅游研讨会的主题是"体验美丽中国、共享发展机遇"。

我曾多次到访中国，留下许多美好的回忆，我自诩不是个鉴赏家，但我极为仰慕中国深厚的文化底蕴、5000年的传统以及热情好客的人民。

美丽中国能给来自五湖四海的游客们带来许多不同的体验。

然而，正如我一直所强调的，让你与众不同的并非是你拥有什么，而是你如何发挥自己的所长，在这方面中国就做得很好，正在努力抓住旅游带来的发展机遇。

中国将旅游列入国家重点发展计划中，这种政治意愿恰是所有旅游政策取得成功的前提。

中国还通过加强监管框架，确保越来越多的民众能享受带薪休假，从而大大增强了出境旅游市场。

此外，中国继续加大对机场、高铁等基础设施和公共交通的投入；这些举措不仅促进国际旅游的发展，同时也推动国内旅游的增长。

朋友们：

现如今，在发达国家和新兴国家，旅游已成为经济、就业、出口和投资的主要驱动力之一。

2013年，全球出境游客超过10亿（准确地说，有10.87亿），旅游消费高达1.4万亿美元，其中所涉及的服务占全世界服务出口的30%，每11份工作中就有一份是旅游业提供的。

2014年前八个月，虽然欧美地区经济复苏缓慢乏力，外加地缘政治不断恶化，但国际旅游却能保持5%的增长速度，这远远超出我们的预期。

在这样的背景下，我们不能忘记亚太地区近年来在国际旅游发展中发挥的作用。

2013年，全球23%的出境游客选择亚洲作为目的地，据联合国世界旅游组织预测，到2030年这个数字将上升至30%。

这些成绩很大程度上要归功于中国，归功于其迅速崛起的中产阶级以及国家对旅游发展的大力支持。

2013年，中国的出境游客达到9800万人，旅游消费合计1290亿美元，超越德国和美国，成为世界最大的客源市场。

另一方面，中国也是入境旅游的领导者。2013年，中国共接待外国游客

5600万，成为全球第四大（前三分别是：法国、美国和西班牙）旅游目的地，其国际旅游收益同样排名第四（前三分别是：美国、西班牙和法国）。

朋友们：

毋庸置疑，近几十年来，中国旅游业已取得巨大进步，与此同时，仍有许多机遇可充分利用。

这些机遇包括推动区域整合与区域内合作，同时也面向欧洲的传统市场和拉丁美洲的新兴市场。

再者，在可持续发展方面，中国具备先天优势，可将自己定位为旅游业的领导者。

在联合国世界旅游组织的支持下，在中国建立的6个全球旅游可持续观测点便是很好的例子。从中，我们可以看出中国为监测旅游影响所做出的努力，以及采取必要措施确保旅游增长与社会责任两不误。

此外，就这方面，请允许我向支持《全球旅游道德规范》的相关人员表示祝贺。

我们必须牢牢记住，旅游在推动经济增长、促进就业、提供发展机遇的同时，也让我们面临更大责任和可持续发展挑战。

所以我很欢迎所有签署《全球旅游道德规范》的新企业，我也相信，联合国大会在2001年核准的这份指导性文件将会增强企业的社会责任感，造福全人类，造福地球。

女士们、先生们，朋友们：

最后，我代表联合国世界旅游组织在此承诺，将继续同中国一道努力巩固旅游作为国家社会经济发展关键驱动因素之一的重要地位。

再一次感谢你们的热情款待，我相信接下来的讨论将有助于我们更深刻地了解中国旅游发展的价值和潜力。

在2014中国国际旅游研讨会闭幕式上的总结发言（1）

杜 江

中国国家旅游局副局长

（2014年11月14日，中国 上海）

女士们、先生们：

大家下午好！经过一天热烈而精彩的研讨，研讨会即将谢幕。在此，请允许我代表中国国家旅游局向出席今天研讨会的各位贵宾、专家、业界和媒体朋友再次表示衷心的感谢！

本次研讨会由联合国世界旅游组织和中国国家旅游局首度联合举办，目的是借助中国国际平台，将世界旅游业的美好未来呈现在世人面前，引导各国、各地区进一步重视旅游业，为其发展创造良好的内外部条件，建立起政府间、政府与业界间、业界与业界间的对话平台，更深入地开展国际旅游交流与合作。从今天嘉宾们发言和讨论的盛况来看，本次研讨会取得了丰硕的成果，达到了预期的目的。开幕式上，中国国家旅游局李金早局长为本次会议提出了重要的建议，也指出了明确的方向。瑞法依秘书长给我们描绘了全球旅游业的美好蓝图。各位演讲嘉宾围绕"体验美丽中国、共享发展机遇"这个主题，从世界旅游发展趋势、旅游品牌营销、游客消费行为分析以及如何促进中国入境旅游持续增长和分享中国出境旅游发展机遇等核心议题做了深入探讨。嘉宾们以专业、敬业的精神，各抒己见，畅所欲言，交流了思想，扩大了共识。研讨会务实高效、成果丰硕，成为中国国际旅游交易会一道崭新、亮丽的风景线。

女士们，先生们，加快中国旅游业发展，加快推动旅游市场一体化，加强国际旅游交流与合作，实现互利共赢、共同发展，是时代的需要、现实的选择，是国内外旅游业界的共同心声。让我们携手共进，共同创造旅游业更加美好的未来！

谢谢各位！让我们相约明年昆明再见！

在2014中国国际旅游研讨会闭幕式上的总结发言（2）

祝善忠

联合国世界旅游组织执行主任

（2014年11月14日，中国 上海）

女士们、先生们，朋友们：

我非常高兴今天有这么多人聚集在这里！

首先，我要感谢中国国家旅游局的辛勤努力和大力支持。我个人也特别感谢杜江先生，他为本次活动成功举办做了大量准备工作。

女士们、先生们：

毫无疑问，我们大家都一致认为，中国国际旅游总体上对世界旅游业产生巨大影响，包括入境旅游和出境旅游，这也是为什么我们今天聚在这里召开本次研讨会。我们是为了中国以及通过广大中国游客与中国互相联系的其他国家的共同利益。正如秘书长所说，中国出境旅游发展已取得卓越成绩。越来越多的中国游客已开始将目光瞄准中东、非洲、太平洋和中欧地区的新兴旅游目的地，同时他们对东南亚、欧洲和美国的兴趣也丝毫不减。前面有些发言人提到了新兴目的地尝试一切办法吸引中国游客，为中国游客提供便利，提供更多的旅游产品，更为重要的是，我们还注意到，大多数目的地都愿意进一步了解中国游客的需求和行为。

女士们、先生们：

银联国际是中国最大的银行业务供应商，对于出国旅游的中国人民，我们希望今天您所看到的一切将让您对中国出境旅游抱有更多美好的愿望。我们建议与会人员可以同各位发言人以及主题研讨会专家们进一步沟通交流，获取更多相关信息。可能有人会说，与出境旅游相比，中国的入境旅游显得相形见绌。但是我想跟大家一起再回顾下秘书长在上午发言中所提到的一些事实，首先，2013年中国仍是世界第四大旅游目的地；其次，中国受北美和欧洲等传统市场的影响；再次，中国凭借其丰富多样的旅游服务、雄厚的东道主能力、完善的基础设施以及强有力的政策支持，完全有潜力成为一流目的地。就今天研讨会而言，我认为中国还应该洞察新兴市场，为今后的发展多一手准备。联合国世界旅游组织目前正在研究旅游便利性、连通性和持续性等议题。那些问题通常都贯穿在旅游发展的过程中，而且所有要素都是实际存在的。

女士们、先生们：

非常感谢你们参加今天的研讨会，我们由衷希望你们都有所收获，也祝愿你们万事如意！在此我还要特别感谢中国国家旅游局和本次研讨会的承办单位。联合国世界旅游组织希望今后有机会参加更多此类活动，更深入探讨中国旅游的热点问题！

谢谢大家！

最后，请允许我利用这个机会再一次感谢所有为本次活动成功举办而付出努力的人员。包括国家旅游局、所有在座单位、所有承办单位以及所有饭店工作人员，感谢所有人付出的努力，非常感谢你们！特别地，也要介绍来自各省的局长，你们今天能够坐在这里听我们介绍中国旅游现状，也是很不容易，非常感谢你们！希望我们明年再有机会在昆明或者某个别的城市，共同再次举办类似的盛会。

中篇
主旨演讲
中国国际旅游的机遇与挑战

美丽中国旅游梦

戴　斌

中国旅游研究院院长

（2014 年 11 月 14 日，中国　上海）

女士们，先生们：

20 世纪 80 年代早期，对于绝大多数的国人来说，旅游是长城、故宫、兵马俑等景区里熙熙攘攘的境外游客。我们从电视画面上、报纸版面上好奇地打量着欧洲人、美国人的金发碧眼，日本人、韩国人精致妆容，港澳同胞、台湾同胞和海外侨胞的时髦衣着。如果各位坐着时光机器穿越到那个时候的中国街道，一定会经常听到"哈喽""老外"的热情招呼声音。那个时候，国人的梦想是能够成为一名导游，会说外语，能挣亲戚邻居很是眼热的外汇券。至于工作、学习之外的旅游离中国人还很遥远，政府主导的旅游发展目标就是赚更多的外汇，以支持国家的经济建设。

20 世纪 90 年代的中后期，旅游是拥挤在景区里看山、看水、看人。中国人第一次拥有可以休息两天的周末，第一次拥有连休七天的"黄金周"，加上改革开放以后近 20 年的经济发展，口袋里多少有了些闲钱，旅游的热情一下子被激发了起来。有钱的坐飞机、住星级酒店，钱少的坐绿皮火车、坐大巴、背着凉白开就出去了。曾经有年轻人裹着军大衣在黄山的山顶上坐了一夜等着看日出，现在想来倒不失为温馨浪漫的青春记忆，真实的情况是游客没有充足的住宿预算，目的地也没有合适的经济型酒店可供选择。

进入 21 世纪，作为国内旅游的自然延伸，越来越多的中国人跨出国境，在欧罗巴好奇地打量着从小就在课堂上知道的埃菲尔铁塔、蓝色多瑙河、威斯敏斯特大教堂,在美利坚实地感受曼哈顿的繁华、潘帕斯草原的辽阔和尼亚加拉大瀑布的壮观,还有新加坡的鱼尾狮、马来西亚的双子塔、香港的红磡体育馆、台北的101大楼,甚至会在北极熊和企鹅的旁边合影。在观光游览的同时,各国各地区精致的商品和远低于国内市场的价格,极大地激发了中国人的购物欲望,以至于中国人被视为"行走的钱包"。因为快速增长的出境旅游,特别是近乎狂热的旅游购物,2009年,中国的国际旅游贸易第一次出现了逆差,并呈不断扩大的态势,预计今年的逆差将会超过1000亿美元。

而今,旅游已经成为老百姓常态化的生活方式,成为"人民群众生活水平提高的重要指标"(习近平,2013)。2014年,中国的国内旅游、出境旅游和入境旅游将分别达到36亿人次、1.14亿人次和1.28亿人次,国民人均出游率达到2.8次。旅游已经成为"现代服务业的重要组成部分"(国务院,2014),我们的目标是到2020年,中国全面建成小康社会的时候,实现人均出游率4.5次,那将是一个60亿人次、5万亿人民币的消费市场,将成为国民经济的战略性支柱产业。国民大众的旅游梦想正在成为"中国梦"的重要组成部分,为此,中国政府和旅游业界正在积极谋划中长期发展战略,并从技术、人才和项目上进行认真的准备。

女士们、先生们:

经过35年的发展,中国正在从大众旅游发展的初期阶段向中高级阶段演化。展望今后的五年,如何让更多的国民能够参与到旅游活动中来,让中低收入的城乡居民能够享受基本的旅游权利,如何让旅游者享受更高的服务品质,却是摆在我们面前的重大现实课题。13亿多人口的大国啊,有人连真正意义上的观光旅游还没有享受呢,有人已经对十万元级的订制旅游挑三拣四了;城里的人想逃离钢筋水泥的丛林,山区和农村的居民想过上城市的现代化生活;有人想多一些、再多一些假期让自己可以实现"想走就走的旅行",还有很多人想获得更多的工作时间，多挣些钱让自己的基本生活能有得到有效的改善。新一届政府宣称，"人民群众对美好生活的向往就是我们的奋斗目标"。作为一名始终关注国民旅游的学者，我欣喜地看到了体现国家意志的《旅游法》、承载政府战略的《国民旅游休闲纲要》《国务院关于加快旅游业改革与发展的若干意见》等文件，为国家旅游发展确定了方向、目标、实施路径和保障手段。由于中央政府明确了发展的信心，各级地方政府不断加大对高铁、机场、高速公路、江河湖海的客运码头等旅游基础设施，以及旅游问询中心、旅游宣传推广、游客满意监测与投诉处理等旅游公共服务的投入，金融资本、产业资本、现代科技应用和年轻人的创业创新，让国民大众的旅游活动有了更多可供选择的市场主体。在这一旅游权利均等化的伟大历史进程中，同样离不开国际资本和旅游业界的合作，中国将以更大的开放力度吸引国际资本、技术和人才投资国内旅游市场，引入新型的旅行服务、酒店管理、主题公园、文化创意、汽车租赁、房车宿营等商业形态。一个开放、多元的旅游产业体系正在加速形成中。

在强调国内旅游基础市场的同时，我们也认识到出境旅游同样是国民旅游权利的重要组成部分，并需要包括中国在内的各国政府和旅游业界的共同努力，以确保高游客能够享受高品质的异地生活体验。事实上，尽管中国承受了越来越大的旅游贸易逆差，但是迄今为止，尚没有迹象表明政府将加大出境市场的管制力度。相反，中国愿意看到旅游目的地国家和地区搭上中国出境旅游繁荣发展的快车，并在教育国民文明旅游方面付出最大的努力。中国国家主席习近平先生就多次谈到出境旅游，在南亚访问时还与游客谈心：不要乱扔矿泉水瓶子，不要破坏珊瑚礁，少吃点方便面，多尝尝当地的海鲜。中国国家旅游局也在反复宣传并引导游客遵守《出境旅游文明公约》。与十多年前走马观光的"高速公路游"相比，今天的中国游客希望深入地体验不同国家和地区的文化与民情，分享高品质的生活方式，并希望能够得到足够的宽容和殷勤好客的对待，能够感受到自己是"受欢迎的中国人"（"欢迎中国""Welcome Chinese"）。中国旅游研究院连续8个季度的中国出境游客满意度调查表明：以加拿大、法国、新西兰、新加坡和西班牙为代表的目的地国家获得了中国游客较高的满意度评价的同时，我的同胞对国际旅游目的地的中文接待环境、中餐、导游、电视、报纸、网络等中文资讯，以及居民的包容度等方面还有颇多抱怨之处。从近期数据来看，由于民航安全、恐怖袭击和接待设施不尽完善等方面的原因，中国游客到访最多的周边国家如马来西亚、菲律宾、印度尼西亚、柬埔寨、越南等，满意度呈下降趋势。有关中国出境游客满意度的进一步资讯，我的同事将在下午的发言将向各位专题报告，大家也可直接从中国旅游研究院咨询获取分国别的完整报告。无论是满意，还是不满意，都是国人的旅游梦想实现过程中阶段性的视角。中国有句老话，"挑的才是买的"，游客的挑剔反映了他们对目的地国家的期待，并希望以此促进其旅游接待环境和服务品质的提升。

在努力满足并不断提升国民旅游需求的同时，政府和旅游业界还致力于优化国家旅游接待环境，想方设法提升入境游客的接待设施和服务水准，真诚地欢迎越来越多的外国人、港澳同胞、台湾同胞和海外华人华侨亲身体验"美丽中国"。经过三十年的高速增长，中国入境旅游的"封闭红利"似乎正在过去，数十亿到访问中国内地的国际游客似乎觉得中国已经不再神秘，而且局部的雾霾天气、短期的食品安全、人民汇率的升值，以及"黄金周"期间的拥堵等印象，让人感觉"中国，想说爱你不容易"。在此，我想和各位分享一个学者眼中的"美丽中国"。中国是一个拥有五千年文明的中国，拥有长城、故宫、兵马俑、京杭大运河和丝绸之路等众多世界文化遗产；中国也是一个正在处于现代化进程中的中国，在上海浦东、北京CBD、深圳前海、苏州工业园、成都春熙路等地，我们可以与全球的时尚同步。中国是一个美丽山水的中国，黄山、张家界、漓江、长江三峡、黄河壶口瀑布，都是世界级的旅游符号；中国也是多彩人文的中国，孔子的一句"有朋自远方来，不亦乐乎"，还有可爱的大熊猫，与五十六个民族相异相融的生活方式，足以让世界各国的游客到中国来可观光、可休闲、可度假、可体验。为了让游客往来更方便，政府采取了取消边境旅游项目审批、分阶段推进外国人72小时过境免签、扩大免税购物场所、开放航权、推动区域旅游合作、互办旅游年等政策举措,来确保国际旅游市场的发展繁荣和稳定增长。我们愿意与国际社会一道,在系统把握旅游发展趋势和游客需求变迁的基础之上,统筹公共部门、私营部门和社会各界力量,为世界各国游客提供更加美好的旅游体验。因为,我们认同并一直在践行这个神圣的理念——"旅游是人人享受的权利"(世界旅游组织,1980)。

女士们,先生们,

中国人的旅游梦想还包括能够"走出去",在世界范围内向游客提供"中国服务"。今天与世界旅游组织签署"全球旅游道德规范"的企业集团都是中国旅游业界的优秀代表,港中旅集团、国旅集团、首旅集团、锦江集团、岭南集团、万达文旅等综合旅游运营商,中青旅、春秋、广之旅、携程、去哪儿等旅行服务商,开元、金陵、华住等酒店运营商,海昌、长隆、乌镇等主题公园和景区投资者,以及更多正在成长中的商业机构,在国内市场获得了相对稳定的竞争优势以后,当然也会遵循商业规则谋划在全球旅游市场的战略布局。可以预计,美丽中国的旅游梦终有一天会成为美丽世界的旅游梦想。在中国的旅游服务走向世界的进程中,我们希望获得各位的认可与支持,就像中国游客今天所获得的礼遇一样。

2008年北京奥运会那句激动人心的口号早已经超越了体育的范畴,回响在包括旅游在内的人类文明进程中:同一个世界,同一个梦想!

谢谢!

世界旅游的发展趋势

徐 京

世界旅游组织亚太部主任

（2014 年 11 月 14 日，中国 上海）

尊敬的各位部长、各位代表、女士们、先生们：

大家上午好！此次回到上海，我的心情无比激动。

首先，同前面发言人一样，我要感谢中国国家旅游局、上海市人民政府以及其他帮助我们筹办中国国际旅游交易会此次研讨会的合作伙伴。

今天，我将在接下来几分钟为大家勾画一张世界旅游发展趋势的宏伟蓝图，希望借此为研讨会的后续谈论抛砖引玉。

女士们、先生们：

正如秘书长先前提到的，当我们审视国际旅游时，大家请看这张幻灯片，我们所谈论的是超过 10 亿的国际游客，可以推算出，平均每天就有超过 300 万游客迈出国门，走向世界，这是一种大规模的活动，也是人类经济史上激动人心的现象。从这种幻灯片上我们还可以看出，2013 年，旅游业仍是全球经济领域增速最快的行业之一。这是旅游业的重要驱动力，是就业的驱动力，更是贸易服务的驱动力。

纵观全球国际旅游全局，我们可以看到，去年亚太地区接待的国际游客人数约为 2.5 亿人次，约占全球国际旅游市场的 1/4 份额。下面，我想和大家分享亚太地区区域旅游的两个统计结果。在游客人数方面，去年东南亚接待的国际游客人数在亚太地区再次排名第一；而在旅游收入方面，东北亚则毫无悬念地位居首位。针对2014年上半年国际旅游的发展趋势，我想特别强调三个地区，那就是美国、亚太地区以及欧洲，它们在2014年的8个月里表现突出，且保持稳定增长态势。

女士们、先生们：

回顾2014年，全世界平均增长率达到4%~4.5%，而亚太地区比全球平均水平高出一个百分点。

中国作为新兴出境市场，其增长速度令人激动，对此我无须过分强调。大家都已经知道，中国早在两年前就形成了全球最大的出境旅游市场。而且在未来几年仍将保持这种强劲增长势头。根据我们的区域预测，我们对现在到2030年的旅游发展充满信心。预计到2030年，全球旅游人数将达18亿人次。其中，亚太地区的国际游客人数将在2013年的2.5亿人次基础上翻一番，到2030年将达到5亿人次，约占全球市场的30%份额。届时，南亚将是全球增速最快的区域，而东北亚将代替欧洲成为全世界接待国际游客最多的区域。

以上所说的数据和事实是关于旅游发展趋势的粗略统计和预测。女士们、先生们，除了这些数据和事实，联合国世界旅游组织还在努力解决一些实际问题，积极应对各种挑战。其中第一个挑战是如何实现签证便利化，目的地的签证政策牵涉到许多问题，联合国世界旅游组织在近两三年也尝试推出一系列的签证政策，并先后在亚太地区、东盟国家以及丝绸之路沿途国家实施。国际旅游社会面临的第二个挑战是税收问题，我们这里说的不是免税，而是理性税收，因为我们发现有许多国家政府轻易就以环保等为由，向我们旅游业强征不公平税收。目前，我们正在努力解决机场税问题，尤其是长途航班的旅客税。

第三个挑战是连通性问题，这个问题我们想要与我们的成员国共同解决。连通性问题在传统意义上通常是指陆地、天空和海洋的连通性，但是，这里我们讨论的是更深层的意义，是旅游带来的社会连通性，以及旅游发展进步带来的技术连通性。

女士们、先生们，

最后，我想简述一下全球国际旅游发展趋势。总体来看，国际旅游局势正在发生转变，其重心确实正从传统的地中海地区和大西洋沿岸转移到亚太地区。

谢谢大家！

中国旅游的品牌传播

何海明

中国中央电视台广告经营中心主任

（2014年11月14日，中国 上海）

谢谢各位！谢谢张司长的介绍！

我利用这个时间给大家介绍一下中国旅游的品牌传播。目前，我国旅游市场欣欣向荣，我们已经是世界第一大出境游第四大入境游消费国，2013年，我国旅游总收入达2.95万亿，直接、间接拉动近1亿人口就业。在媒体传播上，旅游广告量连续5年增长，其中以2013年为优，5年的平均增长率为12%。由此可见，旅游收入、旅游广告、旅游市场呈正相关。在旅游市场中，73%的旅游广告首选电视，电视在中国的覆盖率占人口的98.47%，其他媒体还有电台、报纸、杂志、户外、地铁等，但电视以73%稳居第一。旅游广告的平均投入增速为32%，其品牌效应受到了整个旅游行业的认可。

我们利用这段时间做一下中央电视台播放广告的内容分析。除港、澳、台外，全国31个省市自治区均在中央电视台投放旅游广告。以省为单位来看，这些广告的诉求以各地人文、风景为主，例如西北，基本展现的是大美西北，大美青海，甘肃是河西走廊，宁夏是塞上江南，这是它们以相同点展示不同区域。另外，青海的玉树精神，甘肃的丝绸之路，宁夏的回族风情，则是不同点的展现。我国的西南是多彩的，四川好玩，重庆非去不可，多彩贵州，七彩云南。我们下面可以看一下四川的广告片，四川还有一个标识性的大熊猫形象。此外还有秀丽的华南，活力的广东，清新的福建，广告展现的是各地的人文美景。广东经济比较发达，因而其广告更加全面，它有武术之乡、时尚之都、美食之地。广西主推它的秀美风景，福建这几年一直强调它的清新福建，下面我们看一下福建的广告。这个广告篇幅较短，但其实它有更长的一个版本，我们可能会注意到，广告下面还有信息——各种会议、展会、活动，都会在广告下展现出来。我们再看纷扰的江南，无论是诗画浙江、美好江苏，还是上海，其风景之美自不必说，其格调也是非常的清新。我们注意到，2014年上海主推的是它的迪士尼，浙江主推的是它的西湖博览会，每个地方皆有其主打产品，下面我们看一看浙江的广告。这支广告片比较有代表性，很多省市的广告片格调皆与其相似。中原地区是中华文明的发祥地、厚重中原；好客山东讲的是人和情；晋善晋美——山西也是我们的文明发祥地；燕赵大地——河北；还有河南注重的是河南老家的概念，我们来看看河南的广告。我国东北在北温带上，其天气四季分明，所以我们可以在广告中看到东北春季的纳凉、冬季的滑雪，其广告版本也经常有3~4个，可充分展现其地区差异和季节特色，我们来看一下黑龙江的广告。雪景啊！我们还有几个少数民族地区，如内蒙古、西藏、新疆……其风景壮美，整个广告片皆有民族音乐贯穿其间，令人印象深刻。这些旅游广告展现了当今中国积极进取和欣欣向荣的面貌，我们可从中看到：各省市都在推行其品牌形象。讲到品牌，我想讲三个案例，一个是旅游行业，另外两个属其他行业。

我们首先看一下"多彩贵州"这样一个打造新兴旅游目的地的案例，下面是贵州的宣传片。本宣传片的最后落脚点是"多彩贵州"，它由几个方面来诠释。从片中可以看到，贵州的风景是多彩的，黄果树瀑布、梯田、百里花海、万峰林等；贵州的民族是多彩的，其境内有49个少数民族，各民族共同构建了贵州的多彩文化；贵州的历史是多彩的，遵义会议旧址、四渡赤水等；贵州的产品是多彩的，茅台酒、老干妈、民族织锦等。因此，贵州宣传片的成功不仅在于其出色的广告语，更在于其背后丰富的资源支撑。目前贵州旅游正在央视预算，其宣传片主要投在新闻联播前的提示收看、新闻30分这样的优质资源。2014年1—9月，贵州的宣传片播出了1000多次，累计收看人次达103.8亿。"多彩贵州"不仅是旅游广告,它同时也开发了"多彩贵州"下的不同子品牌,如,多彩贵州的酒、多彩贵州的茶、多彩贵州的艺、多彩贵州的味、多彩贵州的寨等。由此可见,"多彩贵州"是一个内涵丰富的品牌,它将全省的资源都涵括其中,而企业化的管理方式和中心品牌授权体系则使得"多彩贵州"的品牌效果得到了放大。自2010—2013年,贵州旅游收入从1060亿元增长到了2370亿元。众所周知,贵州是我国的欠发达地区,但它靠旅游拉动了全省的经济。总的说来,贵州旅游的成功在于它"多彩"的定位以及围绕这个定位延伸了子品牌,此外,以企业化的管理方式来运营全省旅游品牌以及央视黄金时段的持续性传播也是其成功不可或缺的因素。

接下来我们看第二个案例——农夫山泉,天然水行业第一品牌。其实水这个行业大家都不陌生,我们每个人的生活都离不开水。中国的水行业有两个特征:品种多,纯净水、矿泉水、蒸馏水、矿物质水等;品牌多,娃哈哈、冰露、恒大、百岁山等。那么,农夫山泉是如何在众多的水品牌中脱颖而出,成为行业领导品牌的呢?首先是定位,农夫山泉定位为天然水,国际上并没有天然水的标准,因而农夫山泉可以说是开辟了天然水的品类。所谓天然水既非自来水,也非矿泉水,而是萃取自大自然经过加工的水,如浙江千岛湖的水。为传播并让消费者认知天然水,农夫山泉打出了第一个广告——农夫山泉有点甜,此后它又做了天然水优于其他水的证明——弱碱性实验表明农夫山泉的pH低于同类水,其他营销活动还有很多,如传播农夫山泉是大自然的搬运工和消费者进行寻找水源地的活动。农夫山泉在全国构建了7个水源,浙江千岛湖、吉林长白山、湖北丹江口都包含其中,它还建了11座现代化工厂以作产品生产。此外,农夫山泉非常注重品牌传播,自1998年起,它连续16年在央视黄金时段做广告,2014年更是推出了长达3分钟的寻找水源的长版广告。农夫山泉还积极以多种形式进行品牌渗透,它赞助了央视自1998年开始的5届世界杯以及自2000年开始的4届奥运会的报道,并充分利用冬奥会、纪录片、好歌曲这样的特殊资源以多种形式与消费者见面。经过16年的坚持不懈,农夫山泉现在的销售额超过了100亿，市场占有率超过了24%，是中国日常饮用水的第一品牌。农夫山泉的市场冠军之路在于它开辟了天然水的品类，并进行了与定位相关的营销配称、持续传播和话题营销，它一直是舆论的焦点，消费者也十分接受它。

最后一个案例是极草，它改变了消费者的心智，成了一个品类的代言品。众所周知，冬虫夏草是中国传统的保健品，其传统吃法有打粉吃、煲汤吃、泡水吃，但极草开辟了新工艺，它利用德国技术将冬虫夏草压成100%的虫粉并制成含片，从而开创了冬虫夏草含着吃的新吃法。极草选择的产品传播媒介有三个：央视新闻联播后的黄金时间、民航杂志、户外广告；在表现形式上，极草有3分钟的长版广告，其主要内容为传播含片的服用吸收效果是普通虫草的3到7倍，因而极草具有高效吸收之特性。极草的销售业绩颇佳，从2009年的2000万到2014年的预期60亿，其销售额增长了近300倍。极草营销的成功首先在于它的深度聚焦，它其实面临着很多诱惑——加做其他行业或做虫草的多种形式，但它却始终坚持只做含片这一种产品形式。极草营销成功的第二个原因在于它的精准定位，它以含着吃重新定义了虫草的产品形态。第三，持续在高端媒体上投放长篇广告，且广告本身非常具有说服力。

希望以上贵州、农夫山泉、极草的三个案例能对旅游品牌的营销有所借鉴，也非常欢迎各家旅游品牌到央视来做广告。央视的广告是"一台知天下，登台天下知"。谢谢大家！

中国游客消费行为分析

董 力

银联国际首席品牌官

(2014年11月14日,中国 上海)

尊敬的各位领导,各位来宾,女士们、先生们:

大家好!首先,请允许我代表银联国际和银联国际的首席执行官蔡剑波先生,向各位表示最衷心的感谢和问候!应主办方中国国家旅游局和UNWTO之邀,我非常荣幸地在这里与各位分享银联国际对中国游客境外消费行为的粗浅分析。

银联的国际业务始于2004年。十年来,我们一直致力于为银联卡持卡人提供安全、便捷的跨境支付服务。一方面,我们积极创新,尽量满足中国居民不断增长的境外旅游消费支付需求。同时,通过推动在境外发行银联卡,满足境外人士来华访问、在当地及跨境用卡需求,也为越来越多境外持卡人提供支付服务。

众所周知,如今银联卡已经成为中国人的日常支付工具和出境旅游的标准配置。银联卡不仅能在中国所有POS和ATM上使用,其境外受理网络也拓展至1 300多万家商户和110多万台ATM终端。从全球范围来讲,银联卡拥有包括中国在内的超过2300万家商户和1650万台ATM终端。目前银联卡网络已基本满足了中国游客的境外用卡需求。今天,我主要从银联卡国际业务的角度出发,谈谈当前的旅游消费趋势、中国游客出境游的新特征,以及银联卡在其中扮演的角色。本次汇报主要包括四个部分。

第一,我们来看看目前旅游业的发展大趋势。

加快发展旅游业现已成为很多国家的战略决策。中国政府已把旅游业定位为战略性的支柱产业和现代服务业,并出台《旅游法》以规范市场。美国之前也发布了其国家旅游发展战略,提出了促进旅游业发展的一揽子措施,包括针对中国游客的签证便利化措施等。此外,在经济全球化的带动下,旅游业跨国界、跨领域、跨行业、跨产业、跨部门融合发展的趋势越来越明显。在中国,旅游已经成为人们现代生活的主要休闲方式之一。出境游保持高增长,自由行成大趋势,这些都是引领旅游消费增长的重要领域,而银联卡正在成为中国游客境内外旅游的必备随身物品,几乎所有中国游客皆为银联卡持卡人。银联也一直致力于搭建旅游行业和银行卡产业的交流合作平台,不断提升游客的旅游支付体验。

第二、2014年中国游客出境消费交易的两大特征。

总体上看,2014年中国游客出境消费呈现以下特点:①消费总量规模更大,交易频率更高;②消费行为更加理性。

随着出境游人次规模的进一步扩大,出境消费规模也在持续增长。根据中国国家旅游局预测数据,2014年出境旅游花费将超过1 150亿美元,折合人民币7 242亿元,同比增长超过40%。中国出境游客在境外用卡消费也同样保持着快速增长。随着银联网络服务能力的增强,银联卡支付已经成为中国游客出境消费的首选支付方式。据银联前三季度数据显示,中国游客在境外消费笔数超过1亿笔,交易笔数增速是交易金额增速的两倍。大家可以想象一下,在境外市场,每天有超过一百万次的出境游客用卡消费,这样的规模足以印证一个旅游大国崛起的形象。

在总量规模扩大和频次增高的同时,游客消费特点也发生了变化,其消费渠道更加多元,消费行为更加理性。我们发现,中国游客在境外消费的范围越来越广泛,从过去简单的购物扩展到了度假、休闲、本地化体验等消费,银联卡在日常百货和超市等场所的消费增长较快。这一方面有赖于近年来银联卡在日常消费类受理商户覆盖面的不断扩展,另一方面也与中国游客不再一味购物,而是更多地追求旅游品质并探索当地文化的理念息息相关。

第三，刷卡消费目的地更加分散，用卡范围更加广泛。

除传统的日韩、东南亚等出境游目的地外，中国游客还喜欢去欧洲、美洲、澳大利亚。而在一些新晋旅游热门地，银联卡商户也更加积极地受理银联卡以吸引更多虽非大众但却非常有特点的中国年轻游客。

在传统的热门消费目的地，安全的用卡环境和完善的银联卡受理面进一步助推了中国游客境外消费。以韩国市场为例，今年习近平主席访韩，中韩关系达到新阶段，韩国商户无疑是最大受益者。2014年中国游客在韩国的消费额高速增长，得益于韩国便捷的银联卡支付环境。在明洞、东大门等购物商圈，中国游客均可使用银联卡直接支付。此外中文标示的欢迎语和营销优惠说明也让中国游客在韩国享受到了更加优良的购物体验。

新兴境外消费目的地如希腊、奥地利、土耳其、新西兰等，也越来越受到中国游客的喜爱。在这些地区体验当地生活是中国游客旅程的重点，其消费点往往集中在餐饮和景点。

受《霍比特人》系列电影及《爸爸去哪儿2》热映的影响，越来越多的中国游客将目光投向新西兰。中国人到新西兰旅游已经从低价值的短期购物游逐渐转变为较长时间停留的自由行，自由行游客将成为新西兰市场旅游消费增长的机会。在中国游客到访的热门城镇，如奥克兰、罗托鲁阿、皇后镇等，银联卡的使用非常方便。此外，农庄、文化村、温泉等中国游客喜爱的多元文化旅游景点也迎来了中国游客消费量的快速增长。

第四，银联国际为服务中国出境游客而不懈努力。

10年来，银联卡境外受理商户从2004年的1.23万家增加到2014年的1 300多万家，增长1 000多倍，交易量也从2004年的区区几十亿到现在年复合增长接近80%。由此可看出，银联卡的网络拓展及其服务能力与中国游客出境的规模和增速皆呈正相关。

为了让银联卡持卡人享受更多优惠，银联国际为出境游客准备了丰富的优惠礼遇。2014年,银联国际在全球范围内陆续推出全球60大机场、40大知名商圈和30大旅游胜地营销活动,持续丰富持卡人特惠计划。60大机场活动覆盖全球排名前五的免税集团,以及全球国际客流量排名TOP 20机场中的18家。40大知名商圈活动中,大部分商户针对银联卡的折扣力度统一在10%,有1 000多家商户提供专属折扣。下周即将启动的30大旅游胜地营销活动将更加精彩,届时敬请旅游行业的同人们与银联卡持卡人共同分享。

与此同时,银联品牌在国际市场的知名度和美誉度也不断提升。大家可以在12月初香港举办的亚洲音乐节MAMA看到银联的身影。此外,在新加坡圣淘沙的水幕表演中、在泰国曼谷新天地(Asiatique)的休闲娱乐中、在法国巴黎香榭丽舍大街的亮灯仪式上、在大英博物馆的馆藏纪念手册里,银联品牌都在向世界展示它的精彩与魅力。

近期,我们将与UNWTO一起,在旅游消费研究、优化旅游支付、品牌合作和宣传推广等方面进行合作。另外,我们还将联合中国旅游研究院对中国游客出境消费行为进行深度分析,在不久的将来共同发布"中国游客出境游消费报告"。

最后,再次向中国国家旅游局和UNWTO表示衷心感谢!预祝研讨会圆满成功!谢谢!

下篇
发言与讨论

主题演讲一

入境旅游：如何促进中国入境旅游的持续增长

主持人——杨卫武

上海师范大学旅游学院党委书记、教授

（2014年11月14日，中国 上海）

主持人：

各位来宾，大家下午好！

我是来自上海师范大学旅游学院的杨卫武，下面由我来为大家主持入境旅游的专题研讨。我们这个环节的第一个研讨专题是"入境旅游：如何促进中国入境旅游的持续增长"。

在信息化快速推进的今天，随着信息量的爆炸式增长，游客兴趣的快速多元化，传统的营销方式已经远远不能适应市场发展的需要。借助网络、手机、博客新媒体等来创新营销方式，提升营销效果成为越来越多的国家和目的地入境旅游营销的核心目标。

下面我们就请杭州市旅游委员会的李虹主任来向大家介绍一下，作为中国优秀旅游城市，杭州市在媒体营销方面的成功做法。他的演讲题目是《互联网时代的媒体营销》，有请李虹主任！

互联网时代的媒体营销——杭州旅游营销的经典案例分享

李 虹

杭州市旅游委员会主任

（2014年11月14日，中国 上海）

各位领导、各位嘉宾、女士们、先生们：

大家下午好！首先感谢本次研讨会的主办方给我这个机会，与在座各位分享杭州市旅游委员会在实施面向境外市场的媒体营销的一些思考和做法。

一、新常态新趋势

统计资料显示，2013年，全球入境旅游总人数10.87亿人次，同比增长5%；我国接待入境游客12 907.78万人次，同比下降2.51%，接待入境过夜游客5568.59万人次，同比下降3.53%。入境旅游接待人数增长率从2001—2005年的年均7.91%，降至2006—2010年的年均2.21%，2011年的1.24%，以及2012年的-2.23%。与高速增长的国内旅游和出境旅游不同，入境旅游市场受国内外各种因素影响，下行压力较大。中国入境旅游正经历长期高速发展之后逐渐复归常态化增长的阶段。

我们认为，面对新常态，要理性分析，既要有危机感，也要有信心。就入境市场旅游推广而言，回应需求变化，创新营销理念，依托技术进步，积极实施新媒体和事件营销的智慧营销整合推广，应该是当下最值得思考和跟进的新趋势。

二、互联网时代的政府旅游营销的理论支撑

我们理解,互联网时代的政府旅游目的地营销,其主要内容和目的是基于(移动)互联网、云计算、GPS、大数据、人工智能等新技术,对受众行为和营销效果进行收集、整理和分析,以指导旅游企业或为旅游企业搭建公共资源平台,整合线上线下营销资源,改善营销策略和动作执行,实现精准营销、效益营销的旅游整合营销方式。

线上线下之分具体到媒体类别,也就是所谓的"新媒体和传统媒体"。传统媒体有内容优势,而新媒体有渠道优势。现在的问题是,传统媒体也在做新媒体渠道,而新媒体也在做内容,从形式上看形成内容渠道合一、新旧媒体合一的局面。但实际上传统媒体和新媒体在内容和渠道领域的"专长"还是不一样,这也可以称之为"分工"与"合作",乃至于"竞合(Coopetition)"。伴随着数字和网络技术的发展,受众日益分化和碎片化,他们对不同媒体形式和不同内容的偏向,以及在不同情境下的不同信息消费需求,使得传统媒体与新媒体只有通过融合和互补才能满足不同受众需求。

传统媒体与新媒体的融合使用,同时也是整合营销(Integrated Marketing Communication,简称IMC)的关键所在。IMC理论产生于20世纪90年代,由美国西北大学市场营销学教授唐·舒尔茨(Don Schultz)提出,是指将与市场营销有关的一切传播活动一元化的过程。整合营销传播一方面把广告、促销、公关、直销等一切传播活动都涵盖于营销活动的范围之内,另一方面则能够将统一的传播资讯传达给受众。其中心思想是以通过与受众的沟通满足受众需要为价值取向,确定统一的推广策略,协调使用各种不同的媒体手段,发挥不同媒体的优势,从而以更佳的性价比实现推广高潮。

三、杭州旅委创新旅游营销推广的实践

杭州旅委在2009年就委托亚太旅游组织(PATA)完成了欧美主要市场的

入境市场调研，2010年启动了传统媒体的整合营销。近年来，在此基础上，根据媒体发展趋势对整合营销理论做出完善，全面导入新媒体，并付诸入境旅游市场营销推广的实践。2012年底，杭州旅委积极推进旅游营销智慧化进程，策划了"当代马可·波罗——杭州博士"全球招募活动和以"马可·波罗"为主题的一系列推广营销项目。时间从2013年3月开始持续至今。

（一）夯实基础

在创新城市旅游的营销推广方式的进程中，杭州旅委成立项目小组，不定期召集专家学者、自媒体、业界企业举行群英会，集思广益，发挥民智，就整合营销、新媒体工具的特性等理论进行了深入研究，对海外市场新媒体使用习惯、旅游消费与新媒体的相关性等进行调研。

以整合营销理论为指导，在深入研究、吃透新媒体特点后，杭州旅委确立了新的推广营销方案，精密构建旅游推广营销支持体系，精准定位新媒体营销最佳平台，精心设计"马可·波罗"的主题创意，精确实施带有"杭州基因"的系列活动，精诚维护社交媒体粉丝关系。

（二）策划事件

"事件营销"是攫取注意力资源屡试不爽的手段。"寻找当代马可·波罗——杭州博士"的不同之处是其不止于吸引一时眼球，而是开启了一种长时间、大跨度的事件营销方式。在长达两年的"马可·波罗"旅游推广营销项目中，一个主题贯穿始终，五大阶段有序推进，四部曲环环相扣。

从"甄选"开始，杭州旅委实际上就已经营造了事件营销的氛围，让杭州文化元素和在线互动体验穿插进行，为海外网友提供交互式虚拟体验，让他们了解这座城市，收获独家的"杭州印象"，潜移默化地将城市旅游品牌和价值植入海外受众的心中。

（三）媒体融合

"马可·波罗"系列的营销推广主要借助海外，特别是英文世界，最为流行的四大社交媒体：Facebook、Twitter、Pinterest和YouTube。四大平台各有侧重，相辅相成，其社交属性使得杭州旅游从过去的"集中式广播"，转变为"点对点直播"，让营销面向每一个独立、有再传播能力的人。

与此同时，项目全程辅以线上线下、国内国外、官方民间媒体公关，以"寻找马可·波罗"作为事件营销的焦点，形成传统媒体与新媒体互动，国内与国外平台互动的良好态势。

（四）强调变现

在以"马可·波罗"为主题的一系列营销推广项目实施过程中，杭州旅委对四个海外新媒体平台从零开始，边摸索，边打造，在确保粉丝数量等显性指标完成的基础上，追求互动率、转化率等一些更能体现账户活力和粉丝关系的指标，特别注重探索如何将创新推广与创新营销结合，彼此衔接，通过旅游电子商务实现潜在市场的变现，真正为旅游企业带来新客源。

为推广线上活动，杭州旅委投放了一定数量的互联网广告，以网络联盟形式框选 20 个左右的欧美地区主流旅游相关网站投放各种规格格式的静态广告。广告投放融合互联网语义分析、IP 定向等先进技术，实现精准投放，以最小的预算投入实现了最大的宣传效用。

同时，杭州旅委锁定"机+酒"两大入境旅游必备要素，在境外知名 B2B 公司推广马可·波罗相关活动，建立在线预订渠道，让每一位对杭州产生兴趣的欧美受众能够较为方便和实惠地订到杭州旅游产品，在营销方面找到捷径。

四、杭州旅委的创新旅游营销推广的成效

以"马可·波罗"为主题的一系列营销推广，标志着杭州旅游营销推广全面进入新媒体时代，也为杭州旅游带来了可喜的绩效。

（一）培育了海外杭州粉丝

以"马可·波罗"为主题的一系列推广营销项目，借助海外宣传与国内体验活动的互相链接，将网络新媒体传播方式更好地与境外品牌形象传播相结合，增加杭州旅游品牌的粉丝量和活跃度。

截至 2014 年 10 月，杭州旅游官方账号 Facebook 粉丝 58 583 人，Twitter 粉丝 4 932 人，Pinterest 粉丝 1 599 人，当代马可·波罗活动参与者 25 924 人次（活动于 2014 年 5 月截止）。并且 Facebook 平均互动数达到 100 以上，月平均参与互动人数 3 000 人左右。全国目前有多个城市在海外社交媒体平台上开通了旅游官方账号，杭州旅游的平台数位居第一，粉丝数名列前茅，且粉丝中欧美人群占比甚重，有效提升了杭州旅游品牌在目标网络人群，尤其是欧美人群中的知名度。

（二）突破了营销变现难题

如何实现潜在市场的变现，一直是政府旅游营销推广的难题。在以"马可·波罗"为主题的一系列推广营销项目中，杭州市旅委拨冗去繁，锁定"机+酒"两大入境旅游必备要素，与境外某知名 B2B 电子商务公司合作，推广马可·波罗相关活动。使每一位对杭州产生兴趣的欧美受众能够较方便实惠地预订机票、酒店，提高推广营销活动的转化率。

该 B2B 公司提供的数据显示，仅两个月时间，杭州的酒店预订率同比增长 15%，远高于全国同比增长数值 7%，杭州某酒店预订更是达到 139% 的同比增长率。依靠该 B2B 平台的引流，杭州旅游 Facebook 账号同期也增加了 7 000 名粉丝，社交媒体和旅游预订实现了双涨且幅度极大，可以说是一次非常有效的推广营销创新尝试，成为拉动杭州旅游经济的新力量。

（三）获得了国际业界认可

今年 10 月 10 日，国际权威行业杂志 Marketing 在新加坡圣淘沙举办的年度营销活动，大奖颁奖典礼现场传来喜讯，杭州市旅委策划执行的新媒体旅游营销项目"当代马可·波罗——杭州博士"全球招募活动成功击败了包括联合国基金在内的全球政府机构的逾 400 个参赛项目，获得政府公关活动（事件营销）项目银奖。金奖由澳大利亚皇家海军的国际海上阅兵式（2013 International Fleet Review）夺得。杭州市旅游委员会的该项目同时入围最佳社交媒体应用奖五强。该奖项是国际公认的杰出公关广告行业绩效晴雨表，而且是唯一完全由客户营销人员评选的奖项。

（四）收获了超值公关效益

在"马可·波罗"活动过程中，Forbes、NBC、英国卫报、英国每日电讯、法国费加罗报、美国 Conde Nast Traveller（全球最负盛名的旅游业杂志）、Yahoo US等欧美媒体，以及新华社、人民日报、央视、新浪、腾讯等国内媒体都非常关注，产生了大量的报道和转发。这些报道进一步引发了一些外媒开始主动去搜索了解杭州旅游产业，对杭州旅游进行深入报道，如 US Today（今日美国）等。

根据杭州旅委前期调研和媒体公关经验，美国报纸类主流媒体整版价格约在30万~50万元区间（不含软文撰写费用），按此市场行情计算，杭州在以"马可·波罗"为主题的一系列推广营销项目过程中，至少获得了5 000万元海外公关价值。套用领英（Linkedin）网站《杭州是如何通过55 000美元竞赛来推广旅游的》文章中的一句话："现在提ROI（投资回报率）有些早。但是杭州因此而获得的在传统媒体和新媒体上的曝光，应该是物超所值的。"

五、心得分享

杭州旅委在实施整合营销传播、互联网精准广告定向投放，以及微博、微信运营等项目中，以媒体融合为主要手法进行旅游营销推广，积累了一些经验和体会。

（一）走出宣传局限，树立传播理念

宣传和传播，这两个看似相近的概念，其实有着很大的差别。宣传的行为主体是宣传者本身，是一种"我说你听"的单向传播模式，带有明显的主观性，而传播的行为主体为大众媒体，是以社会媒介的形态出现在大众面前，追求的是客观中立，是一种"你说他说大家说"的多向传播，传播内容平衡兼顾，以受众关心的题材为主，强调客观性，其背后的宣传目的是隐藏的、潜移默化的。

（二）紧跟技术发展，丰富平台种类

Twitter、Facebook 或以视觉分享为主导的 Pinterest、Instragram 正当其道，博客这个已诞生 16 年的媒体似乎已经逐渐被遗忘。而在国内，新浪、腾讯微博大行其道时，微信尚不为人知，时隔一年，微信就已经与微博在用户数上平起平坐。新媒体技术突飞猛进，各类新媒体平台日新月异，对目的地来说，每个平台都是旅游宣传和传播的重要阵地。拥有平台种类越多，受众覆盖面就越广。

（三）灵活平台运用，引入市场机制

平台数量的增加，带来了人力和成本等问题，我们在平台选择上采取了灵活的方式，主要强调资源整合，有效破解了这个问题。集中自有力量打造网站、微博和微信平台，同时采取向市场购买公共服务方式，外包部分新媒体平台尤其是境外新媒体平台业务。通过合同的约束和对服务公司 KPI（关键绩效指数）的考核，不仅把握住了宣传的主导方向，而且引入了市场的竞争和活力，既做到了把宣传融入传播中去，又提高了市场灵敏度，做到了紧跟技术和市场的变化。

（四）线上线下整合，平台相互呼应

线上与线下的全面融合对旅游目的地而言意味着，能脱颖而出的是那些能在最合适的时机、以最合适的渠道，为不同的受众群体提供最合适内容的目的地。许多国外大城市的旅游局投入大量的资源与精力建设在线社交平台，但它们还是会印刷纸质版旅游宣传品。任何一个媒体平台都有其局限性，新媒体平台也是如此。要全年龄层覆盖，只有与传统媒体配合才能达成。同时，不同的新媒体平台其所针对的目标受众也各有千秋，如杭州旅游海外新媒体平台之一的 Pinterest，其受众的 80% 为欧美女性。就国内而言，微博和微信也存在开放和内敛的区别，一些快消品行业在这两个平台的使用形成的"微博撒网打鱼，微信小池养鱼"的经验同样适用于旅游目的地的新媒体宣传。

互联网时代的媒体营销是个动态的、不断创新的演进过程，杭州旅委只是进行了初步的探索，在此与各位分享，敬请不吝赐教，谢谢！

主持人：

谢谢李虹主任的精彩演讲！李主任确实讲得精彩，时间很短，但观点非常清晰。

主持人：

接下来我们有请中国国际旅行社总社有限公司董事长、总裁于宁宁女士就《散客化时代的市场开发与产品创新》与大家交流。大家欢迎！

散客化时代的市场开发与产品创新

于宁宁

中国国际旅行社总社有限公司董事长，总裁

（2014年11月14日，中国 上海）

尊敬的国家旅游局杜江副局长，尊敬的各位领导、各位嘉宾：

大家下午好！很荣幸代表国旅总社和各位领导、嘉宾分享一下入境游散客化时代的市场开发与产品创新。

除1989和2003年外，中国的入境游在1978年到2010年的32年间一直保持着持续的增长，其本质上是受"封闭红利"驱动。中国在外的形象一直是"传统的中国""神秘的国度""和西方世界有着大不同"，这曾使外国游客产生了探知中国的浓厚兴趣并形成了"中国情结"。

然而，自2011年以来，入境游一直处于低迷状态，其影响因素有很多。①海外市场的经济普遍仍处于低迷期，其远程旅游消费需求减少。②中国崛起使得西方国家对中国产生一些误解，西方国家存在对中国的负面宣传。③国内近些年来物价水平的增长和出境游蓬勃发展对入境游构成的机票竞争使得入境游产品价格偏高，超出了外国游客的心理预期。④产品更新较慢，目前入境游旅游产品仍主要为北京、西安、上海、广州、长江三峡旅游路线，加之一些景区、景点的过度商业化开发，入境游的传统原生态元素吸引力减弱。

尽管入境游处于低迷之势，但也呈现出了一些新特点。

（1）游客旅游习惯发生变化，旅游需求升级。随着互联网的普及和移动互联网的兴起，团队游与散客游占比例发生变化并呈现出散客化趋势。中国旅游研究院近期发布的《中国入境旅游发展年度报告 2014》也体现了这一特点。

（2）中国各种旅游基础设施日臻完善，网络服务全面覆盖，智慧旅游程度提升，自助游和自由行的条件已经比较成熟。

（3）"中国魅力"让重游率得以提高。

自 1954 年成立开始，国旅总社的主要业务就是入境游，它可谓见证了中国入境游的整个发展历程。尽管近些年入境游市场发展缓慢，但国旅总社一直坚持着对入境游市场的培育和精心耕耘，时刻做好准备在国家大力发展入境游的新举措下贡献自己的力量，也积极探索散客化时代的市场开发与产品创新。

传统观念过于将散客和团队对立起来。其实，散客也是小团队，只是散客出行的时间和需求更加个性化。散客时代的市场开发与产品创新要关注以下三点：

一、创新入境游运营模式，加强入境游电子商务建设

目前，入境游产品大多依靠国外批发商，在产品研发方面比较被动。直接进入国外的消费者市场，既有利于新产品的开发和推荐，又有利于降低产品成本。当然，直接进入国外散客市场的前期投入会较多，国家可提供相关政策支持散客产品的开发和推荐。针对国外散客市场，除了要加大国内散客接待基础设施的建设，还要提升外国人在中国预订酒店、机票、火车票的方便程度。国旅总社近年来一直把入境游电子商务的发展作为加强入境游散客市场开发的重要手段，不仅建立了多语种的入境游电子商务网站，而且配备了专门的部门和专业团队，面向散客提供包括旅游产品、定制旅游、各类单项产品的预订服务以及友好的网站用户体验，最大程度上为游客提供详尽的中国信息。多语种内容涵盖了旅行各要素并尽可能地开发关联行业，如养生、徒步、骑行、登山、和多种公益活动，这一举措取得了积极成效。

二、创新入境游产品模式，打造"散客成团"产品

目前，国旅总社针对散客市场，积极拓展"散客成团"产品，适应全球游

客不同的出发日期和行程，在目的地进行重新组织和编排，为海外游客的共性需求和个性需求提供差异化服务，把散客成团的路线和目的地不断增加，在散客成团的系列产品中不断增加新的游览内容，取得了较好的效果，散客成团要进一步向规模化方向发展。

三、创新入境游产品内容，深挖旅游目的地的旅游内涵

一方面，拓展新鲜的旅游目的地。除了众所皆知的北京、上海、西安、广州等旅游目的地，国旅总社还在大力拓展新兴旅游目的地，如丝绸之路、大运河、长江三峡、西藏、西南地区等，以期培育市场新亮点。

另一方面，发扬中国旅游产品的精髓，挖掘旅游产品的文化内涵。随着游客旅游经验的日趋丰富，他们对文化体验的要求也日益增加。除经典的世界文化遗产等旅游产品外，国旅总社还将挖掘多元化的文化元素，如美食、音乐、历史、宗教、民俗、园林、古镇等，打造更丰富的文化旅游产品。同时以文化旅游为载体，大力打造深度游。

总之，我们不仅要通过市场开发与产品创新吸引游客来中国，还要吸引游客多次来中国，提升重游率，展现"美丽中国"的更多魅力。谢谢大家！

主持人：

国旅是我国非常棒的一家旅行社，我国的入境游最初就是从国旅开始的。

主持人：

刚才于总给我们做了很好的分析，的确，旅游市场结构在变，我们以前讲"管游客要管住旅行社的牌子、管住导游手中的旗帜"，但现在的情况并非如此。在当前环境下，我国入境旅游市场呈现出怎样的特点呢？

接下来我们有请BBC广告业务大中华区及北亚区副总裁徐倩女士为大家做《BBC关于中国入境旅游报告》。大家欢迎！

BBC 关于中国入境旅游报告

徐 倩

BBC 广告业务大中华区及北亚区副总裁

（2014 年 11 月 14 日，中国 上海）

尊敬的杜局长及各位贵宾：

大家好！非常高兴今天我能够代表 BBC 第三次参加 CNTA 的研讨会。刚才大家在视频中看到的是 BBC 在最近几年的发展及其对中国旅游进行的一系列报道。每年，我们都会把 BBC 最新全球调研数据统计出来，从而给中国入境旅游发展提供一些参考和建议。今天，我们抱着同样的目的来到此次研讨会。

从前面几位嘉宾的发言我们已经看到，中国入境游发展在最近几年有放缓趋势。然而，速度缓则缓矣，真正来到中国旅游的国外游客却是非常富裕，他们每年用于在中国的度假花费达 700 亿美金，其中 63% 的花费与交通无关。1/4 的 BBC 观众在他们上一次旅行中花费 2 500 美金或以上，相当于他们在一次旅行中人均花费 15 000 元人民币。因此，他们来的次数虽不多，但他们每一次的实际消费额以及对中国 GDP 的增长的推动效果非常大。

入境游发展速度的放缓同时也是因为中国周边国家、地区最近在国际营销上的大动作。中国的竞争者包括泰国、马来西亚以及最新崛起的越南，他们在国外媒体上对其文化、城市以及整个国家的宣传，大家都有目共睹。

现在我想讨论一下为什么国际新闻的受众对中国入境游至关重要。

第一，这部分受众不仅是休闲游客，同时也是高端商务游客，是 MICE 会议会展的决策者。例如，BBC 41% 的观众都是商业决策者，他们能够更容易地决定下一次公司会议会展的地点。同时,这部分受众也是意见领袖,78%的观众通常会告知其家人及朋友有关新产品和服务信息,若能影响这部分人群,则营销能够达成多重效果和涟漪效应。此外,我们还有一个非常有趣的数据,75%的欧洲富裕游客没有使用旅行社的计划,而是自行计划国外出游。对于这部分游客,你可以对其进行面对面的直接营销,或通过网络将信息告知他们,让他们直接在网上进行商业采购及旅行计划制订。

BBC的观众有很多都是中国的粉丝。以亚太区观众为例,72%的用户因商务目的来到中国,55%的用户因休闲目的而来到中国。在欧洲区,2013年BBC欧洲地区用户有130万人次到中国游访,在美国,这个数字是210万。这部分观众对中国、对亚洲的关注程度和接受程度很高,因此我们要进一步影响他们,让他们一次、两次、多次地来中国。

我经常会被问道:国外游客会用多长时间来安排他们的旅行计划?通常,国外游客安排旅行计划的时长和他离中国的距离成正比,30%欧洲及美国游客会提前3~6个月开始制订长途旅行计划。在亚洲区,由于距离较近,游客通常提前1~2个月开始制订一个旅行计划,如若有一些周末旅行配套或假日旅行配套,则这部分观众来中国旅游的概率更大。

何时出行?这是另外一个大家都会问到的问题。夏天仍然是美国和欧洲游客度假的高峰期,而亚太地区的观众更容易被吸引在冬天到中国旅行。

国际新闻受众每天随时都可以被影响,他们不仅只用一个媒体,而是像刚才几位嘉宾所言,在一天24小时当中,除了睡觉时间,他们会受到来自不同媒体的不同影响,因此,他们在制订旅行计划时,各平台也会对其决策产生不同作用。例如,国际新闻受众在看电视时可能会被激发灵感并产生旅游欲望,然后他们会使用数字媒体进行具体的调研并完成旅行配套的网络订购。无论是在商务出行期间,还是在度假休闲期间,他们和新闻媒体的结合程度都非常高,92%的观众即使在度假时也会随时随地了解国际新闻,并保持和朋友、家庭的联系。度假时,他们不愿为工作纷扰,所以只有9%的游客表示在度假时想知道

工作情况。

综上所述，国际媒体的新闻受众在整个旅游决策过程中，都与国际新闻媒体时刻保持紧密联系。这对各目的地而言是一个非常好的影响机会。很多游客认为BBC的旅游类节目以及BBC网站旅游频道的内容非常可信且非常有吸引力。对他们来讲，BBC旅游是制定旅行目的地选择的一个非常好的依据。BBC的Travel Show是我们一个值得信赖的旗舰节目，刚才在视频中大家已经看到，我们对中国的很多景点，无论是新的还是旧的，或者鲜为人知的地方，都进行了非常多的报道。2014年，我们对北京的长城特别设立了一个法定涂鸦区并进行了非常有趣的报道，同时，我们也对三亚的阳光、海滩，以及它的森林和国家公园资源进行了深度报道。在网络时代，www.bbc.com/Travel频道在许多观众看来是一个激发旅游灵感的数字平台。2014年，我们对丝绸之路、海南——中国的流浪天堂，以及北京不同凡响的大运河都进行了系列报道。国际新闻媒体受众的时间非常紧张，工作压力也非常大，他们希望能够了解熟知目的地的未知信息，欣赏美丽的照片以及精美的旅游故事，从而激发灵感。即使在上网时，他们也希望能够尽快、轻易地找到一些想找的信息。此外，他们也希望能够了解一些不为人知的目的地。对于他们这部分好奇心，我们在做目的地营销时一定要有所考虑。75%的观众认为，"当我度假时，对我而言最重要的是体验当地真正的文化"。BBC在世界新闻台上对很多国内的旅游基地都进行了大幅度宣传、报道，其中包括72小时免签证过境报道以及对北京、三亚和其他诸多省市旅游局的创意宣传。我们在全球有3.8亿电视用户和7600万网络用户，他们对非常有资历的BBC都非常信任，因此这个平台上发布的鲜为人知的目的地信息或熟知目的地的新信息，都会对他们的旅游订购决策产生极大推动力。

最后，我有三点建议提供给各位目的地营销领导。

第一，国际新闻受众不仅是休闲游客，也是商务游客，我们在传递信息时务必将这两方面因素结合在一起，做到一箭双雕；

第二，国际新闻受众会接受各种媒体的影响，电视以及数字移动媒体在不

同时间对他们产生不同影响;

第三,国际新闻受众对价格因素并不十分敏感,他们对能够激发灵感、鲜为人知、非常漂亮,非常具有灵性的地点更加向往。我们在制订目的地营销方案时要针对这样的富裕高端客户多下功夫,BBC 也愿意与更多的国内旅游局进行合作,帮助大家出谋划策。

谢谢!

主持人:

谢谢徐倩女士的精彩发言!下面我们进入主题研讨环节。

主题研讨一

中国入境旅游的持续增长与推广建议

主持人——杨卫武

上海师范大学旅游学院党委书记、教授

（2014年11月14日，中国 上海）

主持人：

在这个环节我们要请出四位嘉宾，他们分别是：

韩国一般旅行业协会（KATA）副会长、首尔市名誉副市长、韩中商务中心旅行社社长，邹新强先生；

德国迪亚米尔体验旅游公司总经理，马库斯·瓦尔特先生；

印度假日商人首席执行官维卡斯·坎杜利先生；

美国VISA国际组织（亚太）有限公司副总裁，罗斯·杰克逊先生。

有请四位嘉宾上台就座。

四位嘉宾都来自不同国度，而且都一直很关心中国的旅游。鉴于四位来自不同行业，建议邹新强先生、马库斯·瓦尔特先生和维卡斯·坎杜利先生就以下几个方面阐述自己的高见：

（1）从组团社的角度来看，赴华旅游当前依然存在哪些障碍因素有待突破；

（2）从游客视角来看，本国游客对中国的印象与认知状况如何；

（3）从游客视角来看，当前导致赴华旅游满意度下降的突出因素大致有哪些；

（4）从市场特征来看，偏好赴华旅游的游客有哪些基本的行为或者规律特征；

（5）当前和今后一段时期，本国旅游企业，特别是组团社，对中国有哪些期待。

由于罗斯·杰克逊先生来自著名的VISA国际组织，我提议罗斯·杰克逊先生就以下几个方面阐述自己的高见：

（1）境外主要客源市场对赴华旅游的认知与感知评价状况；

（2）中国入境旅游刷卡消费的基本情况；

（3）中国入境旅游刷卡消费当前面临的问题障碍；

（4）境外发达旅游目的地在促进入境旅游刷卡消费方面有哪些成功的案例值得我们借鉴；

（5）为加快中国入境旅游的国际化步伐，增进入境旅游刷卡消费便利性，VISA公司已采取了哪些相关措施，并有哪些成功的经验可以和我们共同分享。

由于时间有限，我建议从邹新强先生开始，每位嘉宾用8分钟时间阐述自己的观点，谢谢！

中国入境旅游市场持续发展的推广方案

邹新强

韩国旅行业协会副会长，

首尔市名誉副市长、韩中商务中心旅行社社长

（2014年11月14日，中国 上海）

女士们、先生们：

大家下午好！我是韩国旅行业协会（KATA）副会长邹新强。在此，我借用张家界旅游产品在韩国的成功营销推广案例来阐述中国入境旅游市场持续发展的推广方案。

除2009年韩国遭遇金融危机外，张家界旅游产品自2005年首次在韩国开发以来一直保持着持续增长。韩国旅行社及韩国公司将张家界旅游产品的主要消费群体定位为40~60岁的人群，并利用下列方案来进行推广活动：

（1）在地铁换乘站设置广告屏幕，在机场或公交车上张贴宣传广告；

（2）在商圈密集区和人流量较大地区使用LED屏幕播放视屏广告；

（3）收集张家界旅游资讯，将其制作成杂志、海报、宣传画册、广告传单等，并散发到主打目标市场中。

为了能够持续推出类似张家界的成功案例，韩国旅行社和韩国公司在中国中央及地方政府的支持下，积极挖掘新的旅游目的地，开发适合新旅游景区特点的商品，并以多种方法进行宣传、推广。值得注意的是，中方在韩国进行宣传、推广的同时需要在景区设置韩文标识和韩文指南，已经设置的指南需做到语意准确，能够为韩国游客所理解，目前不少韩文指南因语意不清而未能发挥

预期作用。

入境旅游市场的持续发展关键在于回访游客。为充分解读景点特色，实现安全旅游，中方需印发多种韩文指南书籍。更进一步，定期举办两国旅游人士和旅行社间的旅游交流会。如：今年8月在韩国举办的为提升中韩旅游质量的合作研讨会及交流大会明年也应该再次举办。

为吸引更多韩国游客赴中国旅游，中方应扩大施行落地签证制度，促进免签制度。

谢谢各位的聆听！谢谢！

主持人：

谢谢邹新强先生！韩国是我国第一大入境旅游客源国，这与韩国旅行协会的大量工作密不可分，我们在张家界确实看到了很多韩国游客。

主持人：

下面有请杰克逊先生！

增进 VISA 刷卡消费，提升中国入境旅游市场的质量

罗斯·杰克逊

美国 VISA 国际组织（亚太）有限公司副总裁

（2014 年 11 月 14 日，中国 上海）

从 VISA 的角度出发，我们关心的是旅游人数以及游客消费量，我们统计的年度旅游报告显示，消费量还未达到全球平均水平，我们还发现，游客选择随身携带现金，这当然一定程度上会限制他们的消费能力。在中国市场，就算是大额消费，有些有钱人也喜欢用现金支付。

我们在近期的调查发现，在接待游客人数最多的三个城市，现金支取总量不断上升。另外，二线城市的基础设施也在不断改善。相关案例研究表明，现金确实有助于游客更好地享受当地美食，欣赏文化特色，也方便他们搭乘交通工具。在中国，饮食占有举足轻重的地位，调查结果显示，如果有更多餐馆和游客喜欢光顾的地方提供刷卡消费，将会推动消费量增长。我们希望在客源市场有所作为，以我们的案例研究为例，我们努力提升远道而来的游客在中国的提现能力，例如与中国相距较远的客源市场——俄罗斯；我们还致力于推动其他市场的轻松支付等关键业务，大家也知道，尚有许多工作亟待完成，我们目前主要集中于部分主要城市及其辖区的一些关键项目，我们利用广大传统、非传统媒体宣传客源市场，在我们看来，与旅游业还有诸多合作机遇。事实上，我们并非推动游客人数的增长，而是帮助游客实现价值最大化。谢谢大家！

主持人：

谢谢杰克逊先生！杰克逊先生从 VISA 卡的刷卡量角度切入，分析了刷卡量成长的原因及其带来的问题，由此对中国入境游客的行为做了很好的分析。

主持人：

德国是我国在西欧最大的国际客源市场。下面我们有请德国迪亚米尔体验旅游公司总经理马库斯·瓦尔特先生。有请！

德国游客对中国的认知变化与散客化趋势下的游客新诉求

马库斯·瓦尔特

德国迪亚米尔体验旅游公司总经理

（2014 年 11 月 14 日，中国 上海）

很高兴有机会在这里和大家分享我们的一些体验。我们是一家旅游运营公司，主要业务是全球范围内的小团旅游和散客游。面向中国的业务对我们公司尤为重要。

我们开展赴华旅游业务已长达 15 年，然而今时不同往日。随着社会不断发展，现在的游客同 20 年前相比已大不相同。在德国游客眼中，中国是个风景秀美、拥有丰富文化遗产的国家，这正是覆盖全球的国际媒体的传播结果。对德国而言，通过媒体宣传旅游是个巨大挑战，即便是在北京奥运会期间，德国许多媒体还是倾向于报道污染、丑闻等新闻，而非运动或是中国的美丽景色，现在的情况也还是差不多。媒体中掺杂了太多政治因素。

旅游业面临的挑战是如何把中国打造成为游客心中安全、现代化的目的地形象。其中，语言问题仍是多年来的老大难，如今即便是在北京、上海这些大城市，游客仍很难与的士司机或是餐馆服务员顺畅沟通。我非常希望在今后几年里，这种现象能够有所改观。

德国游客满意度下降不是因为目的地本身，而是因为他们的需求不断增加，我们的生活发生了巨大变化，对交通或住宿等基本需求远远高于过去 10 年的水平。

以前来中国旅游的德国人大多是 45 岁到 60 岁之间，这方面变化也很大。

如今，来中国旅行的德国人各个年龄段都有。

另外，除了多年来一直占据主流的组团旅游外，新兴的散客游是一种完全不同的旅行方式，对基础设施的需求也大相径庭。

作为旅游从业人员，我们希望为游客提供各种便利服务，以签证便利化为例。还记得14年前我第一次到中国，当时只需要花30欧元，填一份只有一页的签证申请表，而这次我却要花100欧元，填一份多达4页的申请表，整个签证成本增加了300%~400%。我认为这不利于吸引更多游客。所以说，便利的签证至关重要。谢谢大家！

主持人：

谢谢马库斯·瓦尔特先生！

主持人：

下面我们有请印度假日商人首席执行官维卡斯·坎杜利先生。他坐的离我最远，但事实上我们两个国家是挨在一起的。

待坎杜利先生讲完后，我想请四位嘉宾每人再用一句话对中国的入境旅游提些建议。

有请坎杜利先生！

印度游客的偏好特征与当前赴华旅游的障碍因素

维卡斯·坎杜利

印度假日商人首席执行官

（2014年11月14日，中国 上海）

我来自新德里。我们与中国近在咫尺，双方旅游合作潜力巨大。一直以来，中国旅游部门在印度做了很多工作。例如，创建英文网站，我认为这点有很大的帮助。我也认同前面发言人所说的，签证是个难题。虽然它本不应是个复杂的程序，但是留给人们的印象却往往如此。由于沟通不畅，所以业内经营者觉得困难重重。

印度人民对美食情有独钟，有些游客回国后会自豪地向人们说起：我去中国旅行了，我在当地的一家餐馆还自己下了厨。此外，仍有些问题亟待解决。2015年对中国和印度来说都极为关键。在新的一年，要进行目的地规划，届时会奖旅游将会显著增加。

我们需要进一步了解中国，不仅限于北京、上海，我们还想了解中国的其他地方。谢谢大家！

主持人：

谢谢维卡斯·坎杜利先生！我们也真的非常期望中印两国之间的旅游往来做得更多更好。

就刚才所约，我们现在请台上四位嘉宾每人用一句话对中国的入境旅游提一些建议。

邹新强——韩国旅行业协会（KATA）副会长，首尔市名誉副市长、韩中商务中心旅行社社长

非常感谢中国国家旅游局给我这次机会来参加此次研讨会！旅游市场特别大，无论做好做坏，我们都要坦然面对。做好则已，做坏则改。我们不怕发生问题，而怕有了问题却不去解决。我祝愿中国的入境旅游鹏程万里！谢谢各位！

罗斯·杰克逊——美国VISA国际组织（亚太）有限公司副总裁

我们都要遵循客户至上的原则，VISA拥有20亿持卡客户，我们正在努力扫除游客在中国的支付障碍，我认为有一些关键方式可以最大化游客价值，我的建议是，在世界各地实现轻松支付。谢谢大家！

马库斯·瓦尔特——德国迪亚米尔体验旅游公司总经理

在我看来，我们的主要目标是让游客参与其中，而不仅仅是旁观，因为一旦旅行成为他们的生活体验，他们就有可能在未来故地重游。这也是为什么我很想让游客融入当地人生活的方方面面，而不是把他们"分配"到不同的餐馆、酒店，或是那些专为游客准备的场所。这种方式有助于旅游业的可持续发展。谢谢大家！

维卡斯·坎杜利——印度假日商人首席执行官

我认为，印度人不管去哪里，都热衷于购物。比如，他们去瑞士，会买上20千克的巧克力。因为印度人是购物狂，所以购物是否便利就显得尤为重要。

主持人：

刚才四位嘉宾和前一阶段三位嘉宾的观点阐述与思想交锋为我们大家呈现了一场十分精彩的盛宴！我们从中意识到：中国入境旅游的持续增长需要国家

政府从签证、税收、财政、金融、航权、出入境服务配套等综合政策设计等多个角度入手，也需要各级旅游行政主管部门从旅游形象塑造、海外市场宣传、推广等方面下大力气，还需要市场主体和旅游企业在入境旅游产品创新方面多多谋划。此外，市民和游客也需要在这方面共同努力。只有我们共同努力，才能把中国的入境旅游做得更好。让我们再次用热烈的掌声感谢台上四位嘉宾以及前一阶段三位嘉宾的精彩发言！

第一个专题研讨"入境旅游：如何促进中国入境旅游的持续增长？"到此结束！

下一个专题研讨"出境旅游：如何分享中国出境旅游的发展机遇？"将由世界旅游组织亚太部徐京主任为大家主持。有请徐京主任，谢谢各位嘉宾！

主题演讲二

出境旅游：如何分享中国出境旅游的发展机遇

主持人——徐京

世界旅游组织亚太部主任

（2014年11月14日，中国 上海）

主持人：

女士们，先生们：

大家下午好！

下面章节的主题研讨是今天的第二部分。虽然放在后面，但从联合国世界旅游组织角度来看，这个部分是重头戏。出境旅游，尤其是中国的出境旅游，是一个烫山芋。众所周知，中国出境旅游总量已经十分巨大，2014年我国将有1亿人次去往世界各地旅行。在这样庞大的出境旅游总量背景下，非中国人对中国国民出境旅游需求又有多少了解呢？或许你会告诉我，外国人知道中国游客要喝热水，但是，热水之外还有什么需求？今天我们之所以齐聚一堂，讨论中国出境旅游，主要源于中国出境游1个亿的突破量超出了联合国世界旅游组织和其他所有科研机构的预期。在这样的背景下，我们今天利用1个多小时的时间来听听专家们的解读。首先有请中国旅游研究院产业所所长李仲广先生为大家发布《中国出境游客满意度报告》。李先生有请！

中国出境游客满意度报告

李仲广

中国旅游研究院产业所所长

(2014年11月14日,中国 上海)

女士们、先生们:

很高兴由我代表中国旅游研究院"中国公民出国旅游满意度调查"课题组发布调查报告。

一、总体概况

众所周知,近年来中国公民出国旅游人数增长迅猛。为了更好地服务出国游客需求,解决出国旅游市场秩序问题,促进国际旅游合作并为大众旅游背景下的国际旅游发展提供坚实的调研依据和有效工作抓手,中国旅游研究院在中国国家旅游局领导下,自2013年第一季度开展了中国出国游客的满意度专项调查,涉及国外24个主要的中国公民旅游目的地国家。

该调查与另一开展更早、规模更大的"全国游客满意度调查"项目一样,同属中国近年来建设以游客为主的目的地评价体系的基础工程。我们采用的是中国旅游研究院自主研发、设计的游客满意度调研体系,该指标体系建立在期望——感知理论基础之上,还充分吸收了游客在网络上的大量评论意见,该调查体系的科学性得到了国际的认可,在2011年就获得了世界旅游组织的政府创新奖。近两年来,我们针对三万余个游客进行了现场访谈,还收集了一百多万条游客的生动评论,通过细致的研究来发现游客的评价结果。我们已经连续7

个季度做了专题报告的编制、发布和发送工作。

从调查结果来看,中国出国游客总体上是基本满意的。2013—2014年,中国出国游客满意度各季度都持续稳定在75分以上的"基本满意"水平,无论是游客在现场的访谈还是游客在网络上的评论都能够达到75分以上的水平。综合来看,中国游客对国外目的地的综合指标感受良好。近两年来我国公民对国外目的地的城市形象、城市建设、城市管理、公共行业服务和旅游行业服务的平均满意程度分别为81.90、80.95、80.12、80.74、79.81,基本上都处于满意水平。但与此同时也呈现了一些略微下降的趋势,主要体现在自主、自助、自游的这一部分青年群体游客评价有所下降。从游客综合反映的情况来看,游客最为期待的还是中文服务、安全感等方面的大幅改善和旅游投诉满意度的有效提升,包括中文旅游指南、酒店中餐厅、中文电视节目、中文网站、中文客房等服务和中国银联、支付宝设施都是游客需求频率比较高的。

二、目的地国家概况

从24个被调查的国外目的地国家来看,平均而言,第一方阵包括处于80分以上"满意水平"的加拿大、新西兰、新加坡、法国、英国、澳大利亚,新加坡在整个调研监测时间都是有稳步提升的,最近连续两个季度都是稳居在前三名的英国、法国也都采取了持续改善游客体验的政策,包括英国上门签证服务、取消团体游客过境签证等政策,以及法国缩短签证时间、增加景区警力保护等政策和旅游业界增加中国特色餐饮服务等举措。

第二方阵包括处于75~80分之间的"基本满意水平"的美国、西班牙、意大利、日本、德国、韩国、泰国、阿根廷、南非、马来西亚、俄罗斯、菲律宾、巴西、印度尼西亚、柬埔寨,今年以来赴意大利的中国游客满意度也有大幅提升,这与意大利政府和中国旅游研究院共同推进"欢迎中国"发布会有一定关系,中国研究院开展的"欢迎中国"项目是"为中国游客定制"的服务标准体系,目的是与国外目的地的住宿、餐饮、购物、交通、主题公园等商家通力合作，帮助国外商家满足中国游客的核心诉求，意大利罗马机场、意大利新旅客运输公司等单位还获得了"欢迎中国"的认证证书。

仅有三个国家处于75分以下的第三方阵，包括越南、印度、蒙古。从游客的具体评论可以发现，反映比较突出的问题包括中文服务、中文标志、安全感和特色文化方面，例如去蒙古完全感受不到它的特色文化氛围，很多西化的文字完全代替了它原有的一些传统的马头文。

总体看来，24个样本国家的游客满意度得分和排名都是比较稳定的，这也与各个国家的综合国力密切相关，我们将游客满意度得分和人均GDP这两个指标进行综合分析，发现人均GDP处于2万美元的这些国家，其游客满意度指数得分平均都处于78分以上的水平，包括加拿大、新西兰、新加坡、法国、英国、澳大利亚、美国、西班牙、意大利、日本、德国、韩国，人均GDP较低国家的游客满意度指数水平也不高，包括阿根廷、南非、马来西亚、俄罗斯、菲律宾、巴西、印度尼西亚、柬埔寨、越南、印度、蒙古，此外，还有一个表现非常特殊的国家，泰国尽管人均GDP水平不高，但其游客满意度指数排名一直相对靠前，表明中国游客对泰国的旅游服务体验满意程度远远超过了其国家综合基础设施的评价。

三、期望和建议

从2013年中国出国游客满意度调研项目开展实施以来，中国旅游研究院对出国游客满意度进行专项调研和满意度排名，分析研究国外目的地城市的市场环境和公共服务水平，系统、长期地跟踪与分析制约游客满意度的主要因素，定期公布调查结果，为主要目的地城市的旅游质量提升战略提供可资借鉴的中国经验。我们通过驻外办事处与所在目的地的主流媒体建立定期发布机制，向目的地国家和地区的使领馆、旅游推广机构等派发满意度排名和研究报告，并定期组织国内外旅游主管部门、旅游经营机构与旅游研究机构等召开中国出国旅游满意度研讨会。我们建议旅游局、外交部、商务部等政府部门、行业组织在对外交往中都将出国旅游满意度调查结果作为国家对外宣传与交往中的重要内容。我们还与新加坡、意大利等目的地国家和地区建立了游客满意度会商机制。

一个持续增长、健康发展的中国出境旅游市场有利于中国，也有利于世界。随着中国游客对服务品质的要求也越来越高、越来越细，我们建议中国政府和国外目的地国家要共同努力去消除一切不利于民众自由往来的政策壁垒，从点滴的接待细节上善待到访游客，要尽最大努力去保障安全和品质，为游客提供放心满意的旅游体验环境。政府和业界应以互利互惠为原则，简化签证手续、缩短签证时间、减少签证费用，给予出国游客更多的便捷。在语言和消费习惯等方面更加充分地为游客着想，在主要客源集散地和目的地提供更多的中文标识、中文媒体和中文导游服务、银联卡使用，在旅游标准、从业资格互认、安全预警机制和突发事件处置等方面建立起更加紧密的常态化合作机制。建议将出国旅游纳入提升我国文化软实力、推进人文领域交流与合作的战略规划，将出国游客作为国家形象的载体，使国家形象的宣传更加鲜活而生动，将放开中文卫星电视频道落地、更宽松的中文图书报刊进口政策、更为完善的中文接待环境等内容纳入开放和实施中国公民出国旅游的重要条件。

主持人：

非常感谢李所长给我们做的官方分析报告！我希望中国旅游研究院进一步与世界旅游组织的市场部合作，使这一报告不仅在中国得到发布，同时也要让世界各旅游目的地尤其是做中国游客市场的旅游目的地分享这样一个游客满意度报告。

主持人：

听完官方分析报告后，下面有请来自中国专业从事出境旅游咨询机构艾威联合的董事长王新军博士。

王先生有请！

中国出境旅游分析——市场结构和趋势

王新军

艾威联合董事长

(2014年11月14日,中国 上海)

各位领导,各位嘉宾,各位业界同人:

大家好!很高兴有机会在此与大家分享我们对中国出境旅游市场的分析。

在过去10余年,中国出境旅游从起步到快速增长,一定程度上反映了中国社会经济的发展。经过这些年的发展,出境旅行已成为越来越多中国游客的一种生活方式。如果说过去10年是中国出境旅游市场快速发展的黄金10年,那么,从综合评估影响出境旅游的各方因素来看,下个10年仍将是黄金发展的10年,并且是中国出境旅游市场已经转型升级的2.0版本。

首先,我们来看中国出境旅游的客流结构。据测算,2014年中国出境旅行人数有望达1.1亿人次,其中赴港澳地区客流占比70%,赴第三国目的地客流占比30%。在第三国目的地客流结构中,赴亚洲国家客流占比69%,赴欧洲、美洲、大洋洲和非洲等长线目的地客流占比31%。

接下来,我们来看中国出境旅游的客源结构。中国地域辽阔,不同地区经济发展水平也不尽相同。我们按照城镇人口人均GDP以及中产、富裕家庭的数量指标将中国出境旅游客源市场划分为一线、二线和三线三个市场。一线客源市场主要包括中国东部沿海经济比较发达的7个省市(北京、天津、上海、广东、福建、江苏、浙江),这些地区聚集了中国约50%的中产、富裕家庭。一线客源市场目前有1 055家经营出境旅游的旅行社,占全国总出境旅游旅行社比重46%,

这些旅行社组织的出境旅游客流量占全国客流量的66%。二线客源市场主要包括中国广大中部地区的17个省份（黑龙江、吉林、辽宁、内蒙古、陕西、河北、山东、河南、安徽、山西、湖北、湖南、江西、广西、重庆、四川、海南），这些地区聚集了中国约40%的中产、富裕家庭，其城镇人口人均GDP超过5 000美元。二线客源市场目前有1 089家经营出境旅游的旅行社，占全国经营出境旅游旅行社总量47%，其组织的出境旅游客流量占全国客流量的32%。三线客源市场主要包括中国西南和西北的7个省份（宁夏、新疆、青海、甘肃、云南、贵州、西藏），这些地区聚集了中国不到10%的中产、富裕家庭，其城镇人口人均GDP相对较低。三线客源市场目前有165家经营出境旅游的旅行社，占全国经营出境旅游旅行社总量7%，其组织的出境旅游客流量占全国客流量的3%。

从市场发展的特点看，目前中国出境旅游市场正处于转型升级的新阶段，我们认为其有以下几方面的特点和趋势：①出境客流量继续增加，二线客源地区增长潜力大；②游客需求多元化、个性化和碎片化，出境旅游的订制化需求不断增多；③出境旅游运营商和境外供应商的业务定位出现分化，优质供应商将越发受到买家和旅游者的关注和认可；④中国游客境外消费继续增长，但开始趋于理性；⑤自由行市场发展迅速，将从近程周边目的地扩展到中远程目的地；⑥OTA风生水起，行业业态呈现多元化。

去年发布的《旅游法》和《出境旅游优质服务供应商认定与测评标准》也将进一步推进出境旅游市场的转型升级。虽然目前出境旅游市场还面临着一些挑战，但这个市场已经出现了分化，品质旅游的产品也将越来越受到市场的欢迎。中国旅行社协会每个季度都会针对全国50~100家主要出境旅游组团社进行问卷调查。最新调查显示，74%~93%的受访旅行社愿意跟境外优质供应商开展业务合作关系。在针对2015年的出境旅游市场的问卷调查中，中国旅行社总体上表现出乐观的预期：80%受访旅行社预测亚洲游市场将继续增长；82%受访旅行社预测欧洲游市场将继续增长；50%受访旅行社认为美洲游市场将继续增长，也有40%受访旅行社预测美洲游市场2015年发展情况与2014年大体持平；

56%受访旅行社预测大洋洲市场将继续增长；49%受访旅行社预测非洲市场将继续增长，也有41%受访旅行社预测非洲市场2015年发展情况与2014年大体持平，还有10%受访旅行社预测这一市场将会下降。

综合评估影响出境旅游市场的各方面因素，如宏观经济、航空运力、各国推出的签证政策以及各目的地旅游局的大力推广，我们预期：2015年出境旅游市场总体增长率可达10%~15%。

由于时间所限，本次对中国出境旅游市场分析的分享到此结束。作为一家专业从事出境旅游市场研究的咨询机构，我们期待与境内外业界同人有更多的交流。谢谢大家！

主持人：

谢谢王新军博士！刚才我们听到的是两个比较全面的分析报告。接下来的第三位演讲者的演讲是从几个地区部分来探讨中国的出境旅游。有请我的同事——联合国世界旅游组织中东部主任阿姆尔·加法尔先生。他演讲的题目是《非洲和中东开门迎接中国游客》。

有请阿姆尔·加法尔先生！

非洲与中东开门迎接中国游客

阿姆尔·加法尔

世界旅游组织中东部主任

(2014年11月14日,中国 上海)

女士们、先生们,大家下午好,

我非常高兴此次受邀参加中国国际旅游交易会,感谢中国国家旅游局和所有相关单位给我这个宝贵的机会与大家分享中国与中东、北非地区旅游发展趋势和机遇的一些信息和看法。

我的报告主要是关于中国游客赴中东、北非地区旅游的调查研究结果,对此,艾威联合旅游顾问集团给予了宝贵的技术支持。

我还参考了一系列的市场报告、国家季度报告(也叫旅游晴雨表)以及我们的预测研究(《2030年旅游预测报告》),所有这些出版物大家均可在联合世界旅游组织的电子图书馆中查阅。

中东、北非地区包括大约18个阿拉伯语国家,在地理上位于大西洋与印度洋之间,从摩洛哥西部一直延伸到阿曼南部和阿拉伯联合酋长国东部。大家在宣传册封面上就可以看到,两个地区都拥有独特的旅游资源,过去十年里在政府的大力支持以及民营部门的不懈努力下,被精心包装成一系列的核心产品,我们的研究显示,这些产品对中国游客很有吸引力,在今后十年里,很可能会进一步强化产品组合。

下面我回顾一下中东、北非地区旅游发展的主要特征,大家可以从这张示意图上看到相关事实和数据。中东、北非地区旅游业一直保持飞速发展,特别是近十年来，增长率达 11%，几乎是全球平均增长率的两倍，这里我引用的是 2010 年的数据，而在 2011 年初，该地区的地缘政治环境对旅游的快速增长造成负面影响，尤其是在中东地区，虽然这是大势所趋，但整体局势非常危险，因为各地发展极为不均，部分传统目的地受到消极影响，而海湾地区的目的地却呈现加速增长的趋势。

从下面示意图中大家可以发现，旅游业的恢复能力受外部因素影响，北非正在恢复其正增长，而中东则呈现加速增长，但由于行业所受的影响，增速放缓，正持续失去市场份额，不过联合国世界旅游组织获悉的各项指标表明，到今年年底增长速度可能再次恢复。

现在我们来看一看中国游客赴中东、北非地区旅游的主要特征。中国游客赴中东、北非地区旅游市场呈持续快速增长态势。在不到 15 年时间里，旅游人数就从 2000 年的 5 万人次增加到去年的 500 多万人次，仅迪拜酋长国就吸引了超过半数的中国游客。埃及作为传统目的地，其中国游客在 2010 年达到最高峰，此后不断下滑，但目前市场正在复苏。中东、北非地区对中国游客的强大吸引力主要体现在两个方面，一是其历史、文化及独特的遗产，二是其现代大都市设施及服务，尤其是在迪拜、多哈和阿布达比等海湾地区。

前面有几位发言人都提到了一个显著变化，那就是从标准的团队旅游转变到更加个性化的产品和服务，此外，中国与中东、北非地区间不断增加的游客流也对商务旅游产生积极影响，特别是对会奖旅游。

我们的研究还发现，目前有许多因素限制了中国赴该地区旅游市场的发展，这些因素已列举在该图中，第一个是地缘政治环境和中国游客的安全感知，另外，还需提供更多关于目的地和旅游产品的信息，而且航空服务不足或是不便利，例如，阿联酋航空公司主要向中国游客提供前往迪拜或是部分国家的航班。需要进一步拓宽旅游产品的可选范围，以满足中国游客的不同偏好，此外，目前尚缺乏有针对性的宣传，因此在今后应加大宣传力度。

我们的研究还表明，未来短中期（未来五年）市场乐观；迪拜和埃及仍将是该地区的主要目的地；此外，一大批新兴目的地将进入中国市场，例如：摩洛哥、突尼斯和南非，以及约旦和中东。根据预测，商务旅游和公务旅游将显著增长，尤其是海湾地区。

最后，我们的研究还提供了一些如何增加赴该地区中国游客流量的战略方针。针对目的地的成熟度，即知名的、新兴的以及未知的，我们制定了三种不同层次的市场营销策略。例如：提高知名度、产品开发和差异化。提高质量、与中国旅游运营商合作以及打开中国市场。参加交易会和展览会，如本次研讨会，以及开设往返中国航班。我们联合国世界旅游组织将努力推动中国与中东、北非地区间的合作，包括公共部门间合作以及公共部门与民营部门间合作，把握双方旅游市场快速变化的机遇。

谢谢各位的聆听！

主持人：

非常感谢阿姆尔的精彩报告。可能有些人不是很了解MENA缩写指的是中东和北非。所以在我们请出下一位发言人前，我想在这里给MENA做个小广告。我真的很喜欢刚才他所提到一个关键信息，他说到，"这个地区拥有一切"。因为他说的不是中文，所以下面我用中文简单介绍下。

刚才大家听到，我的同事——专门负责中东部的阿姆尔·加法尔主任，介绍了中国游客知之甚少的中东地区和北非地区。他在幻灯片里有一句话叫作"the region has it all"。的确，那块地区虽然鲜为人知，但从旅游目的地角度来讲，它是一个撒满了珍珠的地区。大部分中国游客到中东地区旅游的首选或最后选择就是迪拜，至于文明的两河流域以及同样隶属于阿联酋的阿布扎比，还有约旦、安曼和以前还去的埃及，中国游客踪迹鲜至。所以，我想在这里做一个广告宣传。

接下来，下一个演讲者是来自匈牙利的副国务秘书阿达姆·如辛科先生。他的演讲题目是《中国与中东欧的旅游合作》。有请！

中国与中东欧旅游合作

阿达姆·如辛科

匈牙利经济部旅游事务副国务秘书

(2014年11月14日,中国 上海)

大家下午好(译注:此处发言人用中文问好)!

因为我们在中国有一个很优秀的代表,所以我的中文进步很快。

女士们、先生们:

非常感谢你们邀请我参加本次研讨会,也很感谢你们给我这个机会,让我简单汇报中国与中东欧旅游合作。

我先简短介绍下双方合作历史:2012年4月,中国—中东欧16国经贸论坛在华沙举行,期间中国总理建议成立中国—中东欧国家旅游促进机构与企业联合会。该合作是与中国良好合作关系的体现。旅游协调中心主要研究农业、交通、物流和教育等16个主题,当然,其中一个重要主题是旅游。我们匈牙利有幸领导此次合作。在2014年5月,建立了旅游界第一个合作平台。

我们如何实现合作?2014年5月在布达佩斯共有16个中东欧国家参与建立旅游协调中心,包括:阿尔巴尼亚、波斯尼亚和黑塞哥维那、保加利亚、克罗地亚、捷克共和国、爱沙尼亚、匈牙利、拉脱维亚、立陶宛、马其顿、黑山、波兰、罗马尼亚、塞尔维亚、斯洛伐克、斯洛文尼亚。虽然运营成本由匈牙利政府承担,但是我们仅致力于为所有参与国提供平等权利。

合作包含哪些机遇与利益?中国与中东欧国家在政治、经济与文化领域的合作有着悠久的历史。中国作为中东欧的远途客源市场，目前正快速增长。旅游平台可为中东欧和中国提供机遇，调整旅游产品以适应不同文化的需求，促进知识转移，推动入境旅游，开发新航线以及推出新航班。另外，为了进一步增强中国与中东欧在各个领域的合作，还建立了5个合作平台。

我们的使命和愿景有哪些？中东欧国家应将自己整体包装成一个目的地在中国旅游市场进行宣传和销售。通过共同宣传，推动开发新旅游产品以及特色、利基服务，从而更好地满足赴中东欧中国游客的需要。据预测，在未来十年，中欧地区占中国出境旅游市场份额的比例将增加五倍多。

这里有一些关于中国赴欧洲旅游人数的统计数字

2013年，有750万中国人到欧洲旅游

平均停留时间越来越长

2013年，中东欧成为继西欧之后，接待中国游客最多的地区

共接待250万游客（占中国赴欧旅游人数的33.5%）

到2018年，中东欧国家将接待370万中国游客（增长46.4%）

我们的关键目标是什么？我们需要加强中东欧国家与中国旅游合作，让市场竞争者参与其中，增加中国游客的数量以及停留时间，降低访欧游客的空间集中度，为中国游客提供可靠信息，吸引更加年轻的散客，分享最佳实践，共同开展基于经验的营销活动。

主要的营销工作有哪些？我们必须建立、协调和推进中国国家旅游局与中东欧16国国家旅游局间的合作伙伴关系，创立并交换包括中国和中东欧国家旅游产业名录的数据库，致力于发展新的旅游线路、产品和组合，为合作国的旅游业者提供与旅游签证相关的信息，每年举办一次论坛总结所取得的进展并规划未来活动，加强旅游行业国家级协会或企业间的合作，开通从中国到中东欧地区的直达航班，这点确实尤为重要。

我们在2014年举办了一系列活动，包括联络中东欧16国，为公共网站内

容搜集相关国家信息,发行电子版2013年统计数据刊物(作为对比中国与中东欧国家未来旅游业交易发展的参照基准),参加11月14—16日召开的中国国际旅游交易会,于中国国家旅游局网站建立中东欧国家官方旅游网站页面链接,共享"丝绸之路项目"的新闻稿和照片并以中、英文宣传旅游协调中心目标和活动。

2015年计划开展的活动如下:

在布达佩斯面向国际专业人士召开"中国信息日"会议

在某参与国举办第二届高层年度会议

在线发布2014年旅游统计数据刊物

面向公众的'袖珍指南'移动应用程序在每个国家选取一个旅游景点(区)进行宣传,利用新闻关系,参加2015年中国国际旅游交易会,中国与中东欧旅游展览会目录,高校间旅游教育/知识转移。

谢谢大家!谢谢(译注:此处发言人用中文致谢)!

主持人:

非常感谢阿达姆的精彩报告!我很喜欢你提到的一点。在报告的最开始,你说到,中国国家旅游局是优秀的合作伙伴,这点我和你的想法不谋而合,事实上中国国家旅游局也是联合国世界旅游的杰出合作伙伴。谢谢你提供的建议,也谢谢你一直耐心地在这里陪伴我们。可能大家想看看阿达姆的这篇报告,从打入中国市场的角度来看,这不仅仅是为了宣传而宣传,这还关系到建立一个机构,将中国市场作为客源市场的宣传制度化。这是我们中东欧国家的朋友与中国合作伙伴共同建立的旅游协调中心。基于实证研究展开宣传活动,这可能也是前面其他报告的关键所在。女士们、先生们,我还想跟大家分享另外一件事情,可能你们对我们所选的这位发言人也有所了解。我们没有选择法国、德国或英国等成熟目的地,而是选择了欧洲知名度较低的目的地——东欧国家。下面有请我们的下一位发言人,也是我们本次研讨环节的最后一位发言人,我的老朋友索利亚·亨特女士。她是萨摩亚旅游局局长，更重要的是，她还是南太平洋旅游组织董事会主席。她演讲的题目是"南太平洋岛屿——下一个旅游目的地"，我们之所以选择这个话题，是因为中国游客尚未涉足该区域。下面有请索利亚上台发言。

南太平洋岛屿——下一个旅游目的地

索利亚·亨特

萨摩亚旅游局局长

（2014年11月14日，中国 上海）

借此机会，我要感谢中国国家旅游局和联合国世界旅游组织允许我在这个研讨会上介绍南太平洋。确实，与中国国家旅游局间的良好合作关系让我们受益匪浅，而且中国国家旅游局还是南太平洋旅游组织董事会成员。首先，我先简单介绍下南太平洋旅游组织，它由包括中国在内的16个成员组成，总部设在斐济。

太平洋地区旅游，"游客至上"，我们希望能够尽可能吸引游客，能够理解他们，能够了解他们的喜好，能够与他们建立良好的关系，进而提高客户忠诚度和增进合作关系。

女士们、先生们，我想告诉下大家我们地区有多大。当提到南太平洋时，人们通常会说，噢，那不过是一群没有任何自然资源的小岛，但是，女士们、先生们，我们是下一个目的地，是新目的地，这是为何呢？在我们5 000万平方公里的疆域上生活着1.5亿印第安人。我们正在不断发展壮大，相信你一定会喜欢这里。

我希望大家对我们地区有所了解，请看这些图片，我们拥有绵延数英里的海岸，除了潜水等海洋活动，我们还为游客提供不同的产品，例如：蹦极等。我们的文化中饱含丰富多彩的歌舞表演，例如，大多数人喜欢原创火舞，不过像我们的走火文化，如果你看到了，请勿在家里模仿。除了原创文化外，我们还提供各类酒店和出租公寓,能够满足客人的不同需要。我们5 000万平方公里的疆域上同样也盛产新鲜美食,你们有你们的佳肴,我们也有我们的佳肴,我们尽最大努力保持食物的新鲜度。归根结底,我们在这里分享也是有原因的。我们彼此了解,彼此喜欢,你们了解我们的文化,世界上每个人都能够喜欢我们的文化,这才是旅行的真正意义所在。旅行不是离开自己生活的地方,也不是关于钱,而是了解你们游览的地方,就像我们今天做的一样,我们来到中国,我们享受中国美食。有人可能会说,我都没有谈到关于品牌的东西,确实如此,我们想先知道中国游客的喜好厌恶后,再在国内做相应的调整,所以这也是为什么我们说,在太平洋,"游客至上"。我们有时尚表演,也可以为客人筹备浪漫婚礼。我们也已经享有便利的城市生活,你们拥有的所有便利设施和各种技术我们也都有,例如:我们有多媒体和远程通信能力,大家知道,中国年轻人到哪里都想用智能手机连接Wi-Fi网络上网;还有其他一些工作极具挑战性,我们通过可再生能源发电,建立了高效的电力系统,在未来,还将改善水质,提高与主要客源市场往来的交通便利性,例如:开通新航线、豪华游轮等。也许你们中很多人都认为上述这些理所当然,但对我们而言,着实是费了一番功夫。这其中,挑战重重,也有众多机遇,但我们乐在其中,为什么呢?因为在太平洋地区,我们为所有人着想,我们崇尚安全、健康和友好的环境,而且旅游业的方方面面也需要受过教育的劳动者,需要他们为远道而来的游客提供各种服务。

  人们为什么到我们这里游览?这里的人民友好热情;这里四季温暖如夏,社会治安良好,有原生态的新鲜食物,有趣的文化,独特的活动,手工艺品、艺术、时尚、名牌商品、游戏、运动等一应俱全,游客们既可休闲娱乐,也可尝试冒险活动,享受有意义的旅途,留下难以忘怀的记忆。

  我们确确实实在不断成长,过去五年(2009—2013年)里,中国赴太平洋游客年均增长率达46.4%。在各地区中,斐济的增长率位居首位。

  最后,我想给大家播放一个60秒的小短片。

  请大家观看!谢谢大家!

主持人：

非常感谢索利亚的精彩报告！不管是不是朋友，主持这工作都不好干啊。还是让我们再次以热烈的掌声感谢索利亚。

最后，让我们再次以热烈的掌声感谢所有的发言人，下面，我们有请下一个主题研讨的主持人王新军先生！

主题研讨二

转型中的中国出境旅游——机遇、潜力及挑战

主持人——王新军

艾威联合董事长

（2014年11月14日，中国 上海）

主持人：

大家好！很高兴出境旅游的研讨环节由我来主持。这个环节邀请了6位重量级嘉宾，他们分别来自中国出境旅游组团社、航空公司以及3个目的地国家和一个区域性国际组织。

下面我们有请6位嘉宾上台就座，他们分别是：

中国旅行社总社有限公司副总裁，张士刚先生；

中国国际航空公司市场部总经理，何志刚先生；

新西兰旅游局亚洲区总经理，大卫·克雷格先生；

意大利旅游局亚太区总监，里卡尔多·斯特拉诺先生；

中国东盟中心旅游官员，吴大伟先生；

埃及驻华使馆旅游参赞，阿布博士。

有请6位嘉宾上台就座。

首先感谢6位嘉宾参加今天这个环节的讨论，贡献你们对中国出境旅游市场的真知灼见。我这里有一些问题将分别问到6位嘉宾，请你们就各自问题与境内外业界同人做一些观点分享。

第一个问题提问中旅总社的张总。中国出境旅游发展了这么多年，到目前为止，出境旅游市场与前些年相比有哪些变化，或者说呈现出了什么样的特点？

中国出境旅游市场的新变化与新特征

张士刚

中国旅行社总社有限公司副总裁

(2014年11月14日,中国 上海)

谢谢主持人!

我是中国旅行社总社副总裁张士刚。

就您刚才所问,我想从以下几个方面做一个简要的回答。第一,中国出境游由过去的奢侈消费变成了纯市场化的大众需求;第二,除旅行社和旅游企业外,其他行业,如银行、金融、体育、文化等,都参与到了旅游的行业当中来。第三,出境游产品已经由过去的长途的十几天几个国家的旅游变为短途的单个国家或一两个国家的深度游,出境游向短程化、经济型的方向发展。大家过去可能一至两年出国旅游一次,而现在则可能每个季度或者一旦有假期的时候就想着如何去国外旅游,这种频次的增加使得我国周边国家的亚洲国家目的地更加火爆。此外,过去出境旅游以团体游、组团游方式为主,现在自由行占比越来越大,且自由行方式多种多样,由过去的"机票+酒店"服务增加为自驾游、海岛度假等,这些方式不断地变化。以上是我的回答。谢谢!

主持人:

谢谢张总的分享!目前,全国经营出境旅游的旅行社已达2 300多家,各旅行社都有自己的市场定位或操作模式。那么,请问张总:在新的市场环境下,中旅总社在出境游业务操作模式以及服务品质保障方面都采取了哪些措施?请给我们做一个简要的介绍。

张士刚：

众所周知，中国旅行社总社隶属于中国港中旅集团，中国港中旅集团是中国第一大旅游集团，中旅总社和中国港中旅集团也是中国第一家旅行社。中旅总社一直秉承着服务至上、接待质量优质、价格合理的理念来为社会大众提供服务。首先，作为一家具有历史的旅行社，中旅总社反对低价格竞争，只有不以低价格迎合市场扭曲需求，才能保证客人享受到其应得服务质量，也才能保证市场的规范。其次，2014年中国颁布了《旅游法》，而中旅总社一直非常拥护、支持《旅游法》的贯彻实施。在此过程中，我们在旅游产品规范化、服务质量提升以及引导、规范出境游客文明旅游等方面不断地做出自己的贡献。最后，中旅总社不仅历史悠久，而且还在国内外拥有128家分公司这样庞大的旅行社网络，同时，中旅总社还拥有自己的电商平台——芒果网，这些资源使得我们能够持续跟进社会各阶层游客的需求。此外，无论是我们的旅行社网络还是我们的电商网络，无论是我们对社会销售的产品，还是我们的销售渠道，我们一直是对业内各企业以及社会各市场公开开放的，我们不是自己独立地发展，而是和大家共同成长。以上是我的回答，谢谢！

主持人：

谢谢张总的分享和介绍！

主持人：

我们知道，航空公司是出境旅游市场的重要组成部分，那么，接下来请问国航的何总：站在航空公司的角度，您如何看待中国出境旅游市场的发展潜力？国航明年或未来两年在航线、运力规划方面有没有什么动作，是否可能增设一些新的目的地航线？请何总给我们做一些介绍。

以更优质的航空服务应对中国出境旅游的市场转型

何志刚

中国国际航空公司市场部总经理

（2014年11月14日，中国 上海）

对中国出境游的预测，我相信前台就座的杜局长和戴院长，包括您本人预测得比我们更准一些，但是国航也一直非常关注这些年中国旅游业尤其是出境游的发展。刚才张总已经对中国出境游特点做过介绍，我就不再赘述。在机队规模上，到2015年时，国航将近有82架宽体飞机，这些宽体飞机是能够飞行8小时以上的双通道飞机，因此我们有足够的运力飞往全世界。前段时间德国总理以及APEC期间加拿大总理来到中国时，国航分别和汉莎以及加拿大枫叶航空公司明确了进一步深度合作的意向，由此可见国航仍在国际领域中不断探索。在国内，国航拥有一线、二线和三线市场。可能在大家印象中国航只飞国际线，但事实上国航目前已经是一个大家庭，这个家庭里的成员还有深圳航空、山东航空、澳门航空、大连航空、西藏航空以及内蒙古航空，基本覆盖中国所有内陆和主要城市。经过两年多的融合，国航系正在发挥巨大作用，如今人们无论出境入境皆可通过国航网络自由、方便地进出中国。得益于国家的几个城市的72小时中短免签政策，入境游发展得到了稳步提升，我相信随着政策应用程度的加深，入境游发展会越来越快。出境旅游方面，前面嘉宾提到的目的地，包括历史悠久的中东和一些岛屿地区，确实都非常美丽，我们对其也非常的关注。在不久的将来，国航会在一带一路的国家上开拓新航线，也会在非洲和加勒比海地区开设新航线。谢谢！

主持人：

谢谢何总的介绍！我还想请问您：我国出境游市场正在转型，自助游旅客越来越多，那么，国航有没有什么服务于这部分人群的新产品？或者说，国航有没有针对这一市场与旅行社、目的地旅游局开展一些合作？请谈一下您的看法。

何志刚：

谢谢！其实这两年国航做了很好的探索，我们不断地跟境外旅行社及同业进行合作，并将其目的地介绍给中国公民。例如，国航2014年开航了夏威夷和华盛顿航线，我们与这两个地区的州旅游局及美国联邦旅游局都有很好的合作。当然，我们这么多年也一直与国家旅游局驻他国办事处有很好的合作，如助其推动国家旅游局推出的"美丽中国"。我们期望做一个平台，给国内旅行社出去进行展示的机会。根据目前出境游的特点，国航在机型和客舱产品上做了很大的改善。在最新引进的747-8飞机上，我们设置了4种舱位：针对公务的头等舱和商务舱，以及超经济舱和经济舱。超经济舱非常适合前面所讲的两富一中人群的需求，它不是那么贵，但是非常舒适，关于这些以后有机会我愿意跟各界朋友做进一步分享。谢谢！

主持人：

谢谢何总！谢谢！

主持人：

接下来的问题我想问大卫·克雷格先生。新西兰是中国公民现在去的越来越多的一个国家，2014年赴新西兰的中国游客客流量将近30万。作为新西兰旅游局在亚洲市场特别是中国市场的推广官员，您觉得现在中国游客到新西兰旅游与过去在产品结构方面有什么不同？刚才中旅的张总从组团社角度谈了他们的观点，您作为目的地旅游局代表，又是怎么评价这个市场的发展呢？

新西兰旅游产品的更新与面向中国游客的优质服务

大卫·克雷格

新西兰旅游局亚洲区总经理

(2014年11月14日,中国 上海)

下午好(译注:此处发言人用中文问好)!

是的,你说得很对,中国市场对我们确实非常重要,我们每年都接待近30万中国游客,今年的散客人数更是增加了大约60%,当然,团队游客仍占较大比重。从中我们可以看出,中国游客的偏好发生了很大变化。如今,中国游客想要亲自参与其中,渴望尝试新鲜动物,而不是像过去仅仅满足于观光游览。刚才索利亚介绍了太平洋的蹦极。中国有很多蹦极爱好者,也有许多人喜欢更温和些的活动。在不久前,他们可能会选择去昆士兰州等地的旅游景点,而现在,他们正在全国各地旅行,甚至会去一些不大出名的地方。他们会停留更长时间,过去的停留时间极短,而现在增加了30%左右。他们探索这个国家,开始尝试自驾游,寻找新的住宿方式,这对我们确是一大挑战,我们需要为中国游客设计新的旅游产品。

我们正努力与中国建立持久稳定的合作关系,当然,我们也致力于提供优质服务,我们深知目的地选择的最大驱动因素便是口碑。如果中国游客在新西兰玩好了,就会推荐给他们的朋友,自然就会有越来越多的中国人来我们国家。我们通过与意见领袖保持联系,让他们帮助我们宣传。几年前,也许你们中有些人也知道,我们采访姚晨,她对我们国家一往情深,遂决定在新西兰举办婚礼,这无形中就为我们做了很好的宣传。今年,我们和湖南台的《爸爸去哪儿》

栏目组合作,拍摄了世界上第一部明星和他们子女的真人秀电影,我们希望借此让大家了解到,新西兰不只是个风景秀美的地方,也是个很好玩的地方,在那里,你可以做许许多多的事情。该电影让我们国家在中国市场名声大噪。同时,也启发我们可以将新西兰战略定位为中国家庭游目的地。2015年,我们的目标是一如既往地增强与中国的旅游往来。

主持人:

谢谢大卫·克雷格先生的介绍和分享!

主持人:

今年正好是欧盟国家成为中国公民出境旅游目的地10周年。欧洲一直是中国游客非常向往的远程目的地,其中意大利也是欧洲游的经典。我想问里卡尔多·斯特拉诺先生:您是一位有着非常丰富经验的旅游营销专家,您也代表意大利旅游局在不同国家工作过,在您看来,中国市场跟其他国家的客源市场有什么不同及特点?请您谈谈您的观点和看法。

中国出境旅游市场的特征与意大利的努力方向

里卡尔多·斯特拉诺

意大利旅游局亚太区总监

(2014年11月14日,中国 上海)

非常高兴受邀参加此次研讨会,也特别感谢主办方提供这么好的机会。毫无疑问,每个人都是奔着中国游客来的。对我们来说,意大利只是众多欧洲目的地中的一个,对到欧洲游玩的中国人而言,意大利就像中转站,像一次短途旅行,他们期盼可以做更多事情,却苦于没有时间,这也是为什么我们提倡散客游。你们可能想改变旅游的意义,但我们想成为一个合格的目的地。这意味着我们必须非常努力地工作。在我们的国家,签证仍是个棘手的问题,这里我要自我批评一下,我们下一步的目标是要解决签证问题。另外,有人提到,在中国人们不讲英语,所以我们也必须采取相应措施。中国是个巨大的市场,我们必须慎之又慎,我们的管理工作也必须加倍留心。同时,我们必须不断改进我们的产品,意大利很可能会成为欧洲的主要门户,我们对此有明确的定位。我们也取得了很好的成绩,因为当中国人决定到欧洲旅游时,意大利也在他们的行程安排中,他们对此感到满意。不过,我们还有许多工作要做,我们要满足游客的不同需求和愿望。其次,我们还将鼓励我们的企业家与中国旅游运营商合作。虽然大家都知道中国游客热衷购物,但我们想努力提供更加有保障的购物服务,如果你有机会购物,你会很认真挑选优质商品。因为你没必要浪费自己的金钱和时间,当你即将结束旅行,收拾行囊时,你肯定希望留下美好的记忆,我希望意大利便是你美好的记忆。当你返程时,你渴望将来再有一次这样的旅程，更加深入地了解意大利。这就是我们所谈论的定制产品。对我来说，中国是最重要的市场，我们必须认真对待，谨慎小心。

明年我们最重要的活动是"2015年米兰世博会"，类似前几年的上海世博会，我们期望迎来大量中国游客，因为届时会设有三个中国馆。我们要提高获取信息的能力，抓住有利于意大利的各种机遇。意大利是享誉世界的文明古国，以艺术、美食和美酒、购物闻名。我不希望我的祖国仅仅是个购物目的地，虽然我们生产各式各样的产品，我也承认购物确实极为重要，但如果你尝试更加深入的体验式旅游，你将有机会更好地了解世界。

主持人：

谢谢里卡尔多·斯特拉诺先生！我们也希望明年有更多的中国游客能够到米兰去参观世博会。

主持人：

接下来的问题我想问来自中国东盟中心的吴大伟先生。东盟国家是中国公民出境旅游最早开放的目的地，目前也是中国游客客流量最大的目的地。在您看来，经过这些年的发展，中国游客赴东盟国家旅游还有哪些潜力可以挖掘？此外，这个市场面临什么样的挑战？请您从您的角度谈谈您的观点。

东盟吸引中国出境旅游市场的巨大潜力与面临挑战

吴大伟

中国东盟中心旅游官员

（2014 年 11 月 14 日，中国 上海）

好的，谢谢主持人！

从潜力来讲，东盟国家可以一言以蔽之，即：潜力巨大。"潜力巨大"从两个方面可以看出，首先是硬件环境。东盟国家距离中国较近，其航程较短，价格适中。另外，东盟国家整体来说气候比较温和，适合全年旅游，这对中国游客尤其是中国北方游客具有非常大的吸引力。从旅游资源来讲，东盟国家的自然旅游资源和人文旅游资源都比较丰富，拥有众多的海岛、海滩，以及世界文化和历史遗产。这些都可谓潜力巨大，并且性价比优良。

当然，从另外一个角度来讲，东盟国家仍有许多需要进一步提升的地方。不知道这方面您有没有什么问题？

主持人：

这个市场面临什么样的挑战？从您的角度看，东盟国家在旅游产品结构、服务质量、产品转型等方面有什么可以改进的地方？

吴大伟：

这个问题可以从两个方面来解读。第一，旅游的推广和促销。中国游客比较熟悉的东盟国家旅游产品主要是新马泰这样的经典旅游产品。在相当长的一段时间内，新马泰是中国游客出国旅游的一个敲门砖，在这个基础上，中国游客走得越来越远。其他类似的产品如越、柬沿线产品，这个产品目前正在逐步走向成熟。第二，得益于2011年中国和东盟签署的天空开放政策，双方民用航空路线的开发、开拓已经扫除了政策和技术上的壁垒，我们欣喜地看到，2013年年底时，中国国际航空公司开通了从北京到柬埔寨的航线，现在我们还有北京到泰国清迈的定期直达航班，这对于东盟国家新产品的开发以及旅游客流量的增长具有非常大的推动作用。

主持人：

谢谢！谢谢吴大伟先生给我们的介绍！

我们也注意到，现在越来越多的中国游客开始选择去非洲、中东地区旅游，之前UNWTO的中东部主任也就此给我们做过介绍。埃及也是中国游客的一个重要旅游目的地。我想请问阿布博士：中国市场在埃及整个国际旅游市场中处于一个什么样的位置？另外，经过这些年的发展，特别是从今年以来，我们注意到中国游客到埃及的旅游方式，包括他们的线路选择，都发生了一些变化，请您站在埃及旅游局的角度就此做一些介绍。

独具特色的埃及欢迎中国出境游客到访

阿 布

埃及驻华使馆旅游参赞

（2014年11月14日，中国 上海）

首先，我要特别感谢中国国家旅游局和联合国世界旅游组织邀请我们参加此次研讨会，让我们有机会与大家共同探讨中国出境旅游等议题。

大家下午好（译注：此处发言人用中文问好）！众所周知，中国出境旅游市场正在快速增长，根据之前中国旅游研究院的报告，2014年中国出境游客将超过1.1亿人次，成为世界上最大的出境客源市场。埃及凭借其独特的古代文明，一直是中国游客的理想目的地。因此，我们的旅游宣传包含文化、遗产和文明三大亮点。2013年，赴中东中国游客达到11万人次，其中6.5万人到访埃及，埃及成为中东地区中国游客的最大目的地。

我们通过我们在北京、上海和广州的办事处宣传埃及，另外，我们正努力在天津、青岛和大连等二三线城市建立更多的宣传中心，我们的目标是占据越来越高的中国出境旅游市场份额。

如今，首都开罗是非洲和中东的交通中枢，拥有四通八达的交通网络，连接南非、迪拜、约旦等国家。我们期望在不久的将来接待越来越多的中国游客，当然，我们也会竭尽所能提供更加便利的签证政策、旅游服务和基础设施。

谢谢大家！

主持人：

谢谢阿布博士的介绍！今天关于出境旅游的研讨环节到此结束，谢谢6位嘉宾，谢谢！

Session 1
Opening Remark &
Closing Speech

Opening Remark on China International Tourism Forum 2014 (1)

Mr. LI Jinzao (Chairman of China National Tourism Administration)

(November 14, 2014, Shanghai, P. R. China)

Honorable Mr. Taleb Rifai, Secretary-General,

Mr. Darko Lorencin, Minister of Croatia Tourism,

Mr. Wykeham McNeill, Minister of Jamaica Tourism and Entertainment,

Mr. Muhammad Abdul Kareem Hood, Minister of Sudan Tourism, Ancient Monument, and Wild Animal,

Mr. Safonov, Acting Head of Russian Federal Agency for Tourism,

Ms. Clara Dostalowa, First Deputy Minister for Regional Development of the Czech Republic,

Mr. Adam Ruszinka, Deputy State Secretary for Tourism of Hungary,

Mr. Adolfo Nunes, Deputy State Secretary for Tourism of Portugal,

Asa Medgere, Deputy Minister of Lithuania Economy,

Mr. Cai Dayu, Deputy Minister of Laos News Culture and Tourism,

Mr. Diejo Roman, Deputy Minister of Cook Islands Tourism,

Mr. Rola Anny Adi, Deputy Minister of Fiji Industry and Tourism,

Ms. Sonja Hunter, Chief Executive Officer of Samoa Tourism Authority,

Mykro, Permanent Secretary of Zimbabwe Tourism,

Ms. Kelly Craighead, Executive Director of Travel Office of U.S. Department of

Commerce,

Mr. Gray Kennedy, Lieutenant Governor of Nevada, U.S.

Ladies and Gentlemen,

Good morning! On the occasion of China International Travel Mart (CITM) 2014, the World Tourism Organization (UNWTO) and China National Tourism Administration (CNTA) are co-organizing China International Tourism Forum here. Firstly, I want to give a warm welcome to all honorable guests! Many thanks go to UNWTO and Secretary-General Rifai, and all friends from countries, thanks for your long-term support for tourism development in China!

Today's forum is themed by "Experiencing Beautiful China, Seizing Development Opportunity". To adapt to the changing world, we shall think over and expand tourism cooperation from new perspectives, and exploit huge potential in the tourism industry. Now I'd like to give several suggestions.

I. Jointly discuss the important driving role of tourism development, especially of expanding tourism market, in economic and social development.

At present, global economy is slowly recovered. Tourism, as the largest industry in the world, presents enormous driving force. In 2013, the added value of tourism represented roughly 10% of global GDP, contributing to 3.1% of global economic growth, and directly providing more than 100 million jobs. As the essential component of world tourism, along with the reform and opening up, Chinese tourism, under the correct leadership of the Chinese Government, has developed very rapidly. Tourism has become an important indicator of the improvement of people's living standard, while tourism is developing into a strategic pillar industry of the nation's economy. Chinese President XI Jinping pointed out that tourism is a comprehensive industry, as well as a significant power to advance economic development. Chinese

Premier LI Keqiang stressed accelerating the reform and development of tourism is necessary for upgrading consumption and industrial restructuring. These important judgments correspond to actual situations. It is estimated that tourism contributes to over 40% of retail food and beverage, 50% of culture and entertainment, 80% of civil aviation and railway passenger transport, 90% of accommodations, in the meanwhile, commercial affairs, studying abroad, and many other activities are closely related to tourism, such a comprehensive industry. In addition, at this forum we will also discuss issues like the development stage, approach, and experience of inbound tourism and outbound tourism in different countries, as well as the role of tourism market, and its contribution to economy and society.

II. Deeply discuss the role of tourism development, especially of expanding tourism market, in relationships among countries.

We will discuss the influence of tourism development on bettering and enhancing people-to-people contact and communication. Relationships among countries are actually relations among persons. As the saying goes, "Good relationships among countries rely on close friendship among their people, and the close friendship among the people relies on frequent contact". Without communication, many normal things may develop into misunderstanding, estrangement, or even conflict. For that reason, tourism development can greatly promote the realization of world peace and human common ideal and vision.

III. Jointly discuss basic laws of tourism development, especially of the operation of tourism market, as well as measures and methods to expand tourism market in the new situation.

Every country is developing, but with different conditions, so we shall jointly discuss issues such as how to manage tourism market, how to open up tourist resources, how to employ tourist resources in the context of protection. Most of you are tourism leaders in your countries, and you all have rich knowledge of tourism. This forum is a great opportunity for you to share experience with each other, to contribute to global tourism development.

IV. Discuss international cooperation in tourism circles.

In comparison with other fields, tourism should have the smoothest cooperation. How to use such feature to enhance tourism cooperation? We need to discuss this issue together. We have some cooperation mechanisms about economic and trade regions and sub-regions, but relatively less in the tourism field. Here, we call for the establishment of more, more flexible tourism operation mechanisms, to bring more benefits to tourists and regions where tourist sites are located. To this end, we shall communicate with each other, and go into details.

At last, I wish this forum all success! Once again, thank Secretary-General Rifai and UNWTO officers for long-term support! Heads of tourism of countries and representatives of tourism enterprises, welcome to Shanghai, China! Thank you very much!

Opening Remark on China International Tourism Forum 2014 (2)

Dr. Taleb Rifai (Secretary-General, UNWTO)

(November 14th 2014, Shanghai, P. R. China)

Hon. Mr. LI Jinzao, Chairman, China National Tourism Administration,

Once again, congratulations! We are up to a very good start, it's been a wonderful morning, you can count on our support and our commitment to support you, supporting China, supporting Asia, supporting the entire world tourism community.

Hon. Mr. Du Jiang, Vice Chairman, China National Tourism Administration,

Excellencies,

Ladies and Gentlemen,

Dear Friends.

It is my honor and a great pleasure to be here. I'd like to start with "Nihao" and "Zaoshanghao". I'd like to start by a thank you very warmly to CNTA. You've been an excellent partner, and I want to show this as an example how we can work together. This is the first time that UNWTO contributes to the opening, to the contents and variations to this very important fair.

The theme of China International Tourism Forum 2014 is "Experiencing Beautiful China, Seizing Development Opportunity".

I have had the pleasure of visiting China on a number of occasions and though I cannot claim to be a connoisseur, I am a great admirer of your rich civilization, your millenary traditions and your welcoming people.

A beautiful China with much to offer for tourists from near and far.

Yet, as I always say, it is not what you have but what you do with what you have that differentiates you and in this respect is its clear that China is seizing the development opportunities posed by tourism.

China has placed tourism as one of the priorities of its national development plan and such political will is the first step of any successful tourism policy.

China has also advanced the regulatory framework to allow more and more citizens to enjoy paid holidays giving way to a significant strengthening of its outbound market.

China continues furthermore investing in infrastructure and accessibility both in terms of airports and high speed railways; these development will allow not only to foster international tourism but also to spread tourism within the territory.

Dear Friends:

Tourism is today one of the major drivers of wealth, jobs, exports and investment of advanced and emerging economies.

In 2013, more than one billion tourists (1,087 million to be exact), crossed international borders, spending US$ 1.4 trillion, generating 30% of the world's service exports and creating one in every 11 jobs.

In the first eight months of 2014, despite a lingering economic recovery in Europe and the USA and notwithstanding growing geopolitical challenges, international tourism grew by 5%, way ahead of our expectations.

In this context, we cannot forget the role that Asia and the Pacific has played in the development of international tourism in recent years.

As an inbound region, Asia accounted for 23% of all tourist arrivals in 2013, a share that according to the UNWTO forecasts will increase to 30% in 2030.

And much of these results are due to China, its rising middle class and its support to tourism development.

With 98 million outbound travelers in 2013 and a spending of US$ 129 billion, China is the number one source market in the world, ahead of Germany or the USA.

On the other side, China is also a leader in inbound tourism. With 56 million tourists in 2013, China was the 4th most visited destination in the world (after France, the USA and Spain) and the 4th destination in terms of income generated by international tourism (again after the USA, Spain and France).

Dear friends:

Although there is little doubt that tourism has progressed much in recent decades in China, it is also true that there are many opportunities to continue advancing.

These opportunities include advancing regional integration and cooperation in the region, but also targeting the traditional markets of Europe and the emerging markets of Latin America.

China has furthermore a fundamental opportunity to position itself as a tourism leader in terms of sustainability.

The six Global Sustainable Tourism Observatories existing in China with the support of UNWTO are an example of how the country is committed to monitoring the impact of tourism and implement the necessary measures to ensure that growth and responsibility go hand in hand.

Furthermore, in this respect, allow me to congratulate the stakeholders that have endorsed the Global Code of Ethics for tourism.

We must never forget that with the economic growth, the jobs and the development opportunities that tourism brings, comes greater responsibility and the over-arching challenge of sustainability.

I am thus very happy to welcome all the new signatories of the Code and trust this guiding document, endorsed by the UN General Assembly in 2001, will take your operations to a new level of responsibility to the people and the planet.

Excellencies, Ladies and Gentlemen, Dear Friends,

Allow me to close by expressing UNWTO's full commitment to continuing working with China to consolidate tourism as one of the key drivers of socio-economic development in the country.

I thank you once again for your warm hospitality and I trust that the discussions that follow will provide a very good insight into the value and potential of tourism development in China.

Closing Speech on China International Tourism Forum 2014 (1)

Mr. DU Jiang (Vice Chairman of China National Tourism Administration)

(November 14, 2014, Shanghai, P. R. China)

Ladies and Gentlemen,

Good afternoon! Through one-day good discussion, the forum is coming to an end. Once again, many thanks go to all honorable guests, experts, and media friends.

This is the first time that UNWTO and CNTA jointly host this forum. We aims to, on the strength of China international platform, show all people the beautiful future of world tourism, and lead countries and regions to further emphasize tourism, to create great internal and external conditions for its development, to build dialogue platforms among governments, between government and industry, and among industries, and to deepen international tourism exchange and cooperation. During discussions, thanks to all speakers' wonderful remarks and everyone's active participation, this forum has obtained fruitful achievements and met expected targets. In the opening ceremony, CNTA Chairman LI Jinzao provided major suggestions for this meeting, and also pointed out definite directions. Secretary-General Taleb Rifai drew a beautiful blueprint for global tourism. The speeches of all speakers centered on "Experiencing Beautiful China, Seizing Development Opportunity", including thorough discussions about core issues like world tourism trend, tourism brand marketing, analysis on tourist consumption behavior, as well as how to promote sustainable growth of

China's inbound tourism and share the opportunity of China's outbound tourism. All participants spoke their mind freely, communicated with each other, and reached many new consensuses. This symposium, with pragmatic and efficient style and fruitful outcomes, has become a completely new, beautiful scene of CITM.

Ladies and gentlemen, accelerating China's tourism development, speeding up the integration of tourism market, strengthening international tourism communication and cooperation, and realizing mutual benefit and win-win and common development are requirements of the times, choices of the reality, and common desire of tourism circles at home and abroad. Let's work hand in hand to create a better future for tourism!

Thank you very much! See you in Kunming next year!

Closing Speech on China International Tourism Forum 2014 (2)

Mr. ZHU Shanzhong (Executive Director, UNWTO)

(November 14, 2014, Shanghai, P. R. China)

Ladies and gentlemen, my friends,

I'm really happy to see so many people here today.

First of all, I'd like to thank CNTA for their great work and support. And my personal thanks to Mr. Du Jiang, he has done a great job for this successful event.

Ladies and gentlemen,

There is no doubt that we share the same will that Chinese international tourism , both inbound and outbound, has intensively impacted the world tourism as a whole. That's the reason why we are here with the idea to organize the forum for the benefit of the Chinese as well as the countries interconnected with China through massive Chinese travelers. I'd like to join the secretary general for its outstanding performance in its outbound tourism development. The still increasing Chinese travelers start to explore the emerging destinations in the middle east, Africa, the pacific and the central European while maintaining their interest in southeast Asia, Europe and America. It is hardly to hear the information from the speakers in presenting the emerging destinations they are trying all possible ways to attract and facilitate Chinese travelers, in providing more tourist products, more importantly, we noticed the trend that most destinations are willing to better understand Chinese travelers' needs and behaviors.

Ladies and gentlemen,

UnionPay international is one of the biggest bank providers in China. For Chinese people who are traveling abroad, we hope what's has been brought to you today can provide you more will to Chinese outbound. We do encourage the participants to approach to the speakers and panelists for further information and communication. It may say that Chinese inbound is overshadowed by its outbound. However, I'd like to join you a connotation again to the facts mentioned by secretary general in the morning, first, China is still the fourth tourist destination in the world in 2013; second, Chinese tourism was affected by traditional market such as north America and Europe. Third China has full potential to become a leading destination due to its vast variety of its offering, its capacity as a host, its infrastructure and its policy. From today's forum, I think China should also penetrate the emerging markets for further development. UNWTO is currently working on issues as travel facilitation connectivity and sustainability. Those things are so integrated into the development of tourism in general and all the elements are substantive.

Ladies and gentlemen,

Thank you very much for your participation today and we sincerely hope your participation was a rewarding experience and we wish you all success! I'd like to extend my sincere thanks to CNTA and the sponsors who gave life to the forum. UNWTO looks forward to more forums and activities to further explore the hot topics about China tourism!

Thank you!

Allow me to close by expressing my great gratitude to all persons for this successful activity. I'd like to thank CNTA and all relevant organizations for your great efforts, thank you very much! Particularly, I want to introduce directors from China's provinces. Thank you very much! I hope we will have the opportunity to hold such a great event in Kunming or some other city next year!

Session 2
Keynote Speech
Opportunities and Challenges of China's International Tourism

Beautiful China, Tourism Dream

Mr. DAI Bin (President of China Tourism Academy)

(November 14, 2014, Shanghai, P. R. China)

Ladies and Gentlemen,

In the early 1980s, to most Chinese people, tourism meant sardine-like foreign tourists crowded in such scenic spots as the Great Wall, the Summer Palace, and the First Emperor Qin's Terracotta Army. We saw on television the blond Europeans and Americans, the delicately dressed Japanese and South Korean people, and those fashionably-dressed visitors from Hong Kong, Macau and Taiwan as well as oversea Chinese descendants. If we went back to the former Chinese streets by a time machine, we would often hear the greetings like "hello" and "laowai" (which literally means foreign friend). At that time, a lot of Chinese wanted to be a tour guide who spoke some foreign languages and earned foreign exchange certificates which were the envy of relatives and neighbors. Except in the case of working and studying abroad, the travel or trip for its own sake was still a far-fetched dream. The government-leading tourism was just intended to get more foreign currencies in support of the buildup of the national economy.

In the middle and late 1990s, tourism represented crowds of people viewing mountains, waters and peoples in scenic spots. For the first time, the Chinese people were able to enjoy a two-day's weekend as well as a seven-day' holiday, namely the "Golden Week". What's more, thanks to the economic development in recent 20 years since reform and opening up, Chinese had some spare money, more or less, so that their passion for tourism was sparkled in a flash. The rich travelled by airplane and lived in star hotels, while the poor travelled by green train and bus and took a bottle of cooled boiled water with them. Some youngsters even wore an army greatcoat and sat on the top of Mount Huangshan overnight, just waiting to see the sunrise the next morning. Now we recall that, it is really a romantic memory of the youth. The reality, however, was that tourists didn't have enough money for getting a hotel room while there were no options of proper economy hotels available in the destination.

From the beginning of the 21st Century on, outbound tourism, as the natural extension of the domestic tourism, attracted more and more Chinese people. They went to Europe to curiously watch the Eiffel Tower, the Blue Danube, Westminster Abbey that they already knew in class in the childhood. They went to the United States of America to feel prosperous Manhattan, the vast Pampas Steppe, and the majestic Niagara Falls. They also visited the Merlion in Singapore, Petronas Twin Towers in Malaysia, the Hung Hom Coliseum in Hong Kong, and the landmark skyscraper Taipei 101 in Taipei. They even took a group photo with polar bears and penguins. During the sightseeing, the Chinese tourists also found that oversea commodities were delicate and much cheaper than their counterparts in the domestic market. That had spurred their consumption desire so much that Chinese were referred to as "the walking wallets" abroad. Due to the fast-increasing rush for oversea tours, especially for the fanatic tourist shopping, in 2009 China's international tourism trade saw the first trade deficit. Later, the trade deficit continued to increase, and is estimated to top 100 billion USD this year.

Nowadays, tourism has become a normal way of the public life, as well as "a key indicator reflecting the improvement of people's living standards" (XI Jinping, 2013). In 2014, the domestic tourism, outbound tourism and inbound tourism will respectively reach 3.6 billion, 114 million and 128 million person-times, and the per capita travel rate will come up to 2.8 times. Tourism has become an "important component of modern service industry" (China's Sate Council, 2014). Our goal is that per capita travel rate can reach 4.5 times by 2020 when China becomes a well-off society. And in that case, there will be a six billion person-time market with a tourism consumption of RMB 500 billion yuan, and tourism will become a strategic pillar industry of the national economy. The traveling dreams of the Chinese people are becoming an indispensable part of "the Chinese Dream". To this end, the Chinese government and the tourism industry are taking initiative to work out a middle- and long-term development strategy and are seriously preparing for technologies, talents, and projects.

Ladies and Gentlemen,

Through 35-year development, China is evolving from the preliminary stage of mass tourism to an intermediate and advanced stage. In five years to come, we will have to face major realistic issues like how to make more citizens participate in tourism activities, how to give the basic travel rights to those rural and urban residents with low and medium incomes, and how to make better services available to tourists. In such a country with a large population of 1.3 billion, some people even haven't yet really enjoy a sightseeing trip while some have already been picky about the customized tourism packages worth RMB 100,000 yuan. Urban people want an escape from the jungles of reinforced concretes while rural people and people living in mountains want to live a modern city life. Some hope there will be more holidays that enable their "ever-easy trip" while some hope to get more working time and earn more money so as to effectively improve their minimum life levels. The new Chinese government has declared, "The people's longing for a better life is our goal". As a scholar paying constant attention to the national tourism, I excitedly know we have The Tourism Law-the embodiment of national will, The Outline for National Tourism and Leisure as well as The Opinions of the State Council on Accelerating the Development of Tourism Industry-the representation of national strategies, and other tourism documents. These documents determine the orientation, the goal, the implementing path, and the means of the national tourism development. Since China's Central Government has clarified its confidence in the development, and local governments at all levels have increased investment in such tourism infrastructure as the construction of high-speed railways, airports, expressways, and passenger terminals at lakes and rivers and seas, and in such public services such as tourism inquiry centers, tourism publicity and promotion, tourist satisfaction monitoring, and handling of tourist complaints, strengthened the applications of financial capital, industry capital, and modern technologies, and encouraged the youth's startup and innovation, tourism activities of the public have more optional market entities. The great historical progress of the equalization of the travel right is inseparable from cooperation between international capital and the tourism industry. China will open wider to attract international capital, technologies, and talents into the domestic tourism market, introduce business patterns like new-style tourism services, hotel management, theme parks, cultural creativity, car rental, recreational vehicles, and camping. An open, diversified tourism industry system is forming at an accelerated pace.

While stressing the fundamental tourism market at home, we are aware that outbound tourism is also an essential part of the citizens' travel right, and requires the joint efforts by governments and tourism industry in countries, including the Chinese government, so as to ensure that tourists can enjoy a high-quality life experience in destination. As a matter of fact, in spite of the increasing trade deficit, there is so far no sign suggesting that China will tighten the supervision over the outbound tourism market. On the contrary, China is willing to see that tourist destinations, countries or regions, will share China's prosperity of outbound tourism, and is doing its utmost to educate its citizens to be civilized, well-behaved when travelling abroad. China's President XI Jinping mentioned outbound tourism many times, for example, during his visit to south Asia, XI talked amiably to tourists, "Do not throw water bottles here and there; do not damage the coral reef; eat less instant noodles and eat more local seafood". China National Tourism Administration is also repeatedly promoting and guiding tourists' compliance with The Tourism Etiquette Rules for the Chinese Citizen Travelling Overseas". In comparison with the hurried tour "on the expressway" over a decade ago, today Chinese tourists are expecting to share an in-depth experience of the cultures and folk customs in different countries and regions, to share their high quality lifestyle, and to be treated with adequate tolerance and great hospitality, and to feel themselves the real "Welcome Chinese". According to China Tourism Academy's investigation of eight consecutive quarters on the satisfaction of Chinese outbound tourists, apart from great satisfaction at tourist destinations including Canada, France, New Zealand, Singapore and Spain, tourists made a lot of complaints about Chinese language reception, Chinese food, TV, newspaper, network, and other Chinese information, as well as about the tolerance of local residents in destination. According to recent data, due to the safety problem of civil aviation, terrorist attacks and unsound reception facilities, tourists showed declining satisfaction at these most frequently visited neighboring countries, such as Malaysia, the Philippines, Indonesia, Cambodia, and Vietnam. With regard to the further information of the satisfaction of Chinese outbound tourists, my colleague will give a special report this afternoon. Alternatively, you can directly get the complete reports of different countries from China Tourism Academy. Whether satisfactory or not, these reports provide a phased perspective in the process of Chinese people realizing their tourism dreams. As an old Chinese saying goes, "Buy what you are picky about." Chinese tourists' picky attitude is a reflection of their expectations for the destination country, and by doing this, they hope to improve the reception environment and service quality of tourism.

While striving to meet and upgrade national travel needs constantly, the Chinese government and tourism industry also devote themselves to optimizing the state tourism reception environment and improving the reception facilities and service standards for inbound tourists, sincerely welcoming more and more foreigners, compatriots in Hong Kong, Macao and Taiwan, and overseas Chinese to experience "Beautiful China". After 30 years' high-speed growth, the "close-end bonus" of Chinese inbound tourism now looks like a past story. It seems that billions of international tourists think China is not mysterious any longer. Worse still, regional haze, short-term food safety, appreciation of RMB currency, and traffic jams during "the Golden Week" come to "make it hard for people to say I love you China." Here I want to share with you what the "Beautiful China" is from a scholar's viewpoint. China is a country with a civilization of 5,000 years, boasting the Great Wall, the Summer Palace, the First Emperor Qin's Terracotta Army, Beijing-Hangzhou Grand Canal, and many other world cultural heritages. On the other hand, China is a country in the process of modernization: the fashions of Shanghai Pudong, Beijing CBD, Shenzhen Qianhai, Suzhou Industry Park, and Chengdu Chunxi Road synchronize with global fashion. China is a country with beautiful mountains and waters, possessing such world-class tourism symbols as Mount Huangshan, Zhangjiajie, Li River, the Three Gorges, and the Yellow River's Hukou Waterfall. China is also a country of diversified cultures. We know Confucius said that "Isn't it a great pleasure to have a friend coming from afar?" We have lovely giant pandas, as well as the lifestyle of 56 ethnic groups that coexist in harmony. It is worthwhile for world tourists to come to China for sightseeing, for recreation, for holiday-making and for experience. To facilitate tourists' travel, the Chinese government has revoked the approval of frontier tourism program, promoted the 72-hour Transit without Visa policy phase by phase, expanded the scale of duty-free shops, opened up aviation rights, promoted regional tourism cooperation, and planned the mutual year of tourism. These measures are taken to ensure the prosperity and stable growth of international tourism market. We are willing to work closely with the international community, based on the systematic understanding of tourism development trend and of changes in tourist requirements, to organize the forces of the public/private sectors and social organizations to give world tourists a better travel experience while maintaining the. As a result, we agree with and have always been exercising this holy philosophy-"Tourism activity is everyone's right" (World Tourism Organization, 1980).

Ladies and Gentlemen,

The Chinese tourism dream also includes the ability to "go global", that is, to provide "the Chinese services" to tourists worldwide. These who have signed with World Tourism Organization the Global Code of Ethics for Tourism today are representatives of the excellent Chinese tourism companies, including China Travel Service (HK) Group Corporation, CITS Group Corporation, Beijing Tourism Group, Jin Jiang International, Lingnan Group, Wanda Cultural Tourism, and other integrated tourism operators; CYTS, Spring Airlines, CGZL, Ctrip, Qunar, and other tourism service providers; New Century, Jinling, Huazhu, and other hotel operators; Haichang, Changlong, Wuzhen, and other theme parks and sights investors; and more growth business organizations. These companies have gotten stable competitive advantages, and will for sure comply with business rules and plan a strategic pattern in global tourism market. It can be predicted that the tourism dream of the beautiful China will turn into the tourism dream of the beautiful world. While Chinese tourism service is going global, we hope for your acceptance and support, just like the Chinese tourists being treated with hospitality and politeness today.

The encouraging slogan for Beijing Olympics 2008 has already gone beyond the scope of sports, reverberating in the process of human civilization including tourism: One World, One Dream!

Thanks!

World Tourism Trend

Mr. XU Jing (Director of regional programme for Asia and Pacific, UNWTO)

(November 14, 2014, Shanghai, P. R. China)

Honorable ministers, distinguished delegates, ladies and gentlemen,

Very good morning to all of you! Please allow me for a few minutes before you take your second coffee, let me start by expressing how happy I am to be back in Shanghai.

I want to first of all to echo the previous speakers, I thank you our gracious host, the China National tourism Administration, and also the government of Shanghai, and all the partners who has helped us in the preparing this important symposium within the framework of the CITM.

Today, I'd like to use the next few minutes to provide a broad picture of the trends of international tourism as we speak and hope the few minutes will set the scene for the subsequent librations of today's symposium.

Ladies and gentlemen,

As you heard earlier from my secretary general, when we look at the international tourism, what's the total volume as we speak, you can see from this slide, we are talking about over one billion international travelers, the fact indicates that every single day, we are talking about almost 3 million travelers are crossing their national borders to the rest of the world, this is a massive movement, this is a very exciting phenomenon of economy of our mankind. When it comes to the result of 2013, this slide once again shows that this sector of the tourism industry continues to be one of the fastest growing economic sectors of the world. This is a great driving force of tourism, driving force for job creation, and driving force, more importantly, for trading services.

Within the global picture of international tourism, when it comes to Asia and Pacific for last year, what we can see is that, when it comes to numbers, last year, we received roughly 250 million international travelers, this roughly represents 1/4 of the total global market share of international tourism. I'd like to share two points when it comes to the regional tourism of Asia and Pacific. No.1 if we look at tourism arrivals, one particular sub-region stands up, that is the South east Asia, and this was the once again the star performer last year, while in the same time, in terms of tourism income, it is the sub-region of north-east Asia that is no doubt as another star performer within the A&P. Let's look at the first half year of 2014, I'd like to highlight 3 regions, namely, the America, A&P and Europe, that perform and grow steadily with strong performance for the eight months of 2014.

Ladies and gentlemen,

Look at the entire year of 2014, towards the end of this year, we are talking roughly about world average of growth rate of 4-4.5%, and again within that average, A&P will perform 1% higher than the world average.

There is no need for me to over emphasize the exciting growth rate of China as a specific the emerging outbound market of the world. As you already knew, China became No.1 outbound tourism market even 2 years ago. And this strong trend will continue to grow in the coming years. Briefly, I'd also like to share with you when it comes to the future, if we look at tourism towards 2030, we are very confident according to our regional forecast. By the year 2030, we shall reach the number of international tourists as high as 1.8 billion travelers around the world on the year to year basis. And within the global picture of the future, if we look at A&P by then, it covers 250 million international tourists within the regions that travels will more or less doubled into 500 million international tourists, in another words, this 500 million international tourists in the A&P region will take roughly 30% of the global market share by the year 2030. Again by then, the sub-region of South Asia will be the fastest growing sub-region of the world, while Northeast Asia will be the most visited region of the world instead of concentration of European regions.

There was about roughly tourism trends, about figures and facts. Ladies and gentlemen, when we look at trends, it's not only about facts, it's not only about data, UNWTO also tries to address some issues in order to face the changes. And they are about the issue of visa facilitation, when we talk about visa facilitation, there are many issues related to opening a destination when it come to visa policy, UNWTO in the recent 2-3 years has explored a series of visa policies, first on APEC region, following with another region of ASEAN countries, and then the silk road countries. The second issue as a challenge for the international tourism community relates to the issue of taxation, and we are not talking about not any taxation, but the intelligent taxation, because we feel our tourism industry is still an easy target for many national governments to levy unfair taxation to our industry using excuses such as environmental protection, especially we have been trying to address the issue of airport taxes especially related to long-haul passenger tax.

The third major issue we'd like to address together with our member states is the connectivity issue. Conventionally, the issue of connectivity usually related to the connectivity of road, air and sea, however, we want to go one step further, the connectivity is also related to social connectivity through tourism and it also related to technology connectivity through the development and promotion of tourism.

Ladies and gentlemen,

Finally I'd like to conclude my presentation by indicating that this world international tourism trend. The shift is taking place, the central gravity is indeed shifting from the conventional Mediterranean, the ocean of Atlantic to this part of the region.

Thank you very much for your kind attention!

Brand Promotion of China's Tourism

Mr. HE Haiming (Director of Advertising Centre, CCTV)

(November 14, 2014, Shanghai, P. R. China)

Thank you! Thank Director-General Zhang for introduction!

I'd like to take this opportunity to share with you some information about brand promotion of China's tourism. Currently, tourism market in China is thriving, and China has become the number one outbound tourism country and the number four inbound tourism consumption country in the world. In 2013, China's tourism enjoyed the total revenue of 2.95 trillion, directly and indirectly creating jobs for almost 100 million people. With regard to media promotion, tourism advertisement has grown for five successive years, with a year-on-year growth rate of 12%, and reaching a peak in 2013. It can be seen that, tourism revenue, tourism advertisement, and tourism market are directly proportional to each other. In tourism market, 73% of tourism advertisement depends on TV, the TV coverage reaches 98.47% of the population in China, and there are also other media such as radio station, newspaper, magazine, outdoors, and metro, but TV ranks first firmly on the strength of its proportion of 73%. The investment in tourism advertisement grows by 32% on average, and other brand effects are recognized by the whole tourism industry.

I'd like to use the next few minutes to analysis the contents of advertisements played by CCTV. Except Hong Kong, Macao, and Taiwan, the other 31 provinces/ municipalities/autonomous regions all put tourism advertisements on CCTV. As to different provinces/autonomous regions, their advertisements focus on human culture and scenery, for example, the northwest region is broad and beautiful: Qinghai is broad and beautiful; Gansu is the Hexi Corridor; Ningxia is the Abundant Place outside the Great Wall, and these advertisements show the same feature of different places. In addition, the advertisements also present the differences, for example, Qinghai's Yushu spirit, Gansu's Silk Road, and Ningxia's Hui people. The Southwest region is colorful: Sichuan is very interesting; Chongqing is your destination. There are also colorful Guizhou and colorful Yunan. Please allow me to show you the publicity video of Sichuan: Sichuan possesses a panda logo. There are also pretty South China, energetic Guangdong, and brisk Fujian. Advertisement aims to show human culture and beautiful scenery in various places. As Guangdong is developed, its advertisement is more comprehensive, including City of Kung fu, City of Fashion, and City of Food. Guangxi highlights its beautiful scenery, and Fujian has stressed its "brisk Fujian" in recent years. I'd like to use the next seconds to show you the advertising video of Fujian: this is relatively short, actually it has a longer version. We can notice that, information about conferences, exhibitions, and events are also displayed below the advertisement. Let's look at riotous Jiangnan: picturesque Zhejiang, exquisite Jiangsu, and Shanghai all have beautiful scenery and fresh style. We notice that, in 2014 Shanghai highlights its Disney, Zhejiang emphasizes its West Lake Expo, and each place has its main product. I want to show you the advertising video of Zhejiang: this video is typical of those of many other provinces and municipalities. The Central Plains is the cradle of Chinese civilization, so there is generous Central Plains; hospitable Shandong is about human and affection; Shanxi, a Land of Splendors—Shanxi is also the birthplace of our culture; Yan and Zhao Great Land—Hebei; while Henan highlights the idea of Henan hometown, and this is Henan's promotion. Northeast China is located in the north temperate zones, and has four distinctive seasons, so from the advertisement we can see people enjoy cool air in spring and go skiing in winter, and there are often three to four versions of promotion, to fully display regional differences and seasonal characteristics. This video is about Heilongjiang, what a beautiful snow scene! We also have several areas inhabited by ethnic minorities, such as Inner Mongolia, Tibet, and Xinjiang. The promotion videos of these places present magnificent scenery and contain incidental ethnic music as well, impress people deeply. All these advertisements reflect the aggressive and prosperous atmosphere in today's China. We can also find that: provinces/municipalities/autonomous regions are advertising their brand image. With regard to brand, I want to talk about three cases, one belongs to tourism, and the other two belong to other industries.

The first case is to create the emerging tourist destination of "Colorful Guizhou". This is the promotion video of Guizhou. The highlight of this advertisement is "Colorful Guizhou", which is interpreted in several aspects. It can be seen from the video that, Guizhou's scenery is colorful: Huangguoshu Waterfall, terrace field, Hundred Mile Azalea, Wanfenglin, etc. Guizhou's ethnic groups are colorful: in Guizhou there are 49 ethnic minorities jointly contributing to colorful culture. Guizhou's history is colorful: Site of Zunyi Conference, Crossing the Chishui River Four Times, etc. Guizhou's products are colorful: Maotai, Lao Gan Ma, ethnic brocade, etc. The success of Guizhou's promotion video relies not only on the outstanding advertising words, but also on Guizhou's abundant resources. At present, Guizhou tourism is making a budget in CCTV, and its advertisement is put in such superior resources as "Next Program" before Xinwen Lianbo and in NEWS 30'. From January to September 2014, Guizhou's advertisement was played over one thousand times, reaching 10.38 billion person-times. "Colorful Guizhou" is not only a tourism advertisement, and also develops different sub-brands, including wine of colorful Guizhou, tea of colorful Guizhou, art of colorful Guizhou, taste of colorful Guizhou, village of colorful Guizhou, and so on. In this sense, "Colorful Guizhou" is a brand with rich contents, and includes resources throughout the province, while the corporate management mode and the brand system have enlarged the brand effect of "Colorful Guizhou". From 2010 to 2013, the income of Guizhou tourism increased from 106 billion to 237 billion. As everyone knows, Guizhou is a less developed region in China, but it successfully drives the economy of the whole province by tourism. Generally speaking, the success of Guizhou tourism depends on its positioning of "colorful" and extended sub-brands; moreover, it is also essential that Guizhou operates tourism brand in corporate management ways and uses the prime time of CCTV to advertise continuously.

The second case is Nongfu Spring, the number one brand in the natural water industry. In fact, we are all familiar with the water industry, as nobody can live without water. China's water industry presents two features: a wide variety of water, including pure water, mineral spring water, distilled water, mineral-added water, etc; a wide variety of brands, such as Wahaha, Ice Dew, Hengda, Ganten, etc. But how could Nongfu Spring stand out from other many water brands and become a leading brand in the industry? The first strength is positioning. Nongfu Spring defines itself as natural water, and as there are no international standards of natural water, the initiative of Nongfu Spring has created the new variety of natural water. The so-called natural water is neither piped water nor mineral spring water, but it comes from nature and has been processed, such as water from Thousand-islet Lake in Zhejiang. To give publicity to natural water, Nongfu Spring launched the first advertising slogan—"Nongfu Spring, a little sweet"; later, it did an alkalescence experiment to prove that natural water is better than other kinds of water, as the pH value of Nongfu Spring is lower than that of its counterparts. The company had also conducted many marketing campaigns, for example, advertising that Nongfu Spring is only the porter of nature, looking for water-head together with consumers, and other activities. Nongfu Spring has built seven water sources throughout the country, like Thousand-islet Lake in Zhejiang, Changbai Mountain in Jilin, and Danjiangkou in Hubei. It has also founded 11 modern factories to produce products. What is more, it pays great attention to brand promotion, for example, since 1998, it has put advertisement in the golden time of CCTV for 16 successive years, and in 2014 even launched a three-minute advertisement of looking for water-head. Nongfu Spring also accomplished brand penetration in many ways, for example, it sponsored the broadcast of five World Cup tournaments on CCTV since 1998 and four Olympic Games since 2000, and took full advantage of special resources, such as Winter Olympic Games, documentary film, and good song, to meet with consumers on different occasions. Through untiring efforts for 16 years, now Nongfu Spring enjoys the sales amount of over 10 billion, taking more than 24% of market share, and has become the number one drinking water brand in China. In a word, the market champion of Nongfu Spring depends on its original category of natural water, marketing positioning, and sustained promotion. Nongfu Spring is always the focus of public opinion, while consumers accept it as well.

The final case is Very Grass, which changes consumers' thinking and has become a model product. As you know, Aweto (Dong Chong Xia Cao) is a traditional Chinese dietary supplement. There are also several traditional ways of eating it, including make it into power, stew it with soup, or soak it in water. Very Grass, however, employs new technique: it uses German technology to compress Aweto into 100% larva powder and make it into tablet, so that consumers can smoosh it. The Very Grass product is promoted through three media: prime time after CCTV Xinwen Lianbo, civil aviation magazine, and outdoor advertisement; it has a three-minute advertisement, mainly telling that the Very Grass tablet can be absorbed efficiently—with an absorption effect three to seven times as efficient as ordinary Aweto. Very Grass has obtained excellent sales achievement, increasing from 20 million in 2009 to the expected six billion in 2014, with a growth rate of nearly 300. The success of Very Grass, firstly, relies on its focus, although the company faces a lot of temptation—engaging in other industries or developing other forms of Aweto, it always insists on the tablet form. Secondly, the company grasps precise positioning, redefining the product shape as Aweto for smooshing. Thirdly, it constantly puts long-time advertisement on high-end media, and the advertisement itself is persuasive.

I hope these three cases, Guizhou, Nongfu Spring, and Very Grass, will be valuable to the promotion of tourism brand. And your tourism brands are always welcome to CCTV. The slogan of CCTV is "One station, One world". Thank you very much!

Analysis on the Consumption Behavior of Chinese Tourists

Mr. DONG Li (Chief Branding Officer, UnionPay International)

(November 14, 2014, Shanghai, P. R. China)

Honorable leaders, friends, ladies, and gentlemen,

Good morning! Please allow me to express the greatest gratitude and wishes of UnionPay International and CEO CAI Jianbo to all of you! Thank CNTA and UNWTO for inviting me. It is my honor to share with you the analysis of UnionPay International on the consumption behavior of Chinese outbound tourists.

UnionPay started to engage in international business in 2004. Over the past decade, we have made great efforts to provide UnionPay card holders with safe, convenient cross-border payment service. On the one hand, we actively innovate, to meet the increasing demand of consumption payment for Chinese outbound tourists. On the other hand, we also issue UnionPay card in foreign countries, to provide the payment service for overseas card holders in China and their own countries.

As everyone knows, nowadays UnionPay card has become daily payment tool and standard configuration of Chinese people. UnionPay card can be used on all POS and ATMs in China, and also supported by over 13 million service suppliers and more than 1.1 million ATMs in other countries. Globally, UnionPay card covers over 23 million service suppliers and 16.5 million ATMs throughout the world, including China. At present, the network of UnionPay card is basically able to satisfy the overseas consumption need of Chinese tourists. Today, I'd like to, from the perspective of international business of UnionPay card, analyze current tourism consumption trend, new characteristics of China outbound tourism market, and the role of UnionPay card. My following presentation can be divided into four parts.

Firstly, let's look at current tourism trend.

Now, many countries have made accelerating tourism development as their national strategy. The Chinese Government has taken tourism as a strategic pillar industry and modern service industry, and released Tourism Law to regulate market. America also has introduced its national tourism strategy, and put forward a series of measures to promote tourism development, such as visa facilitation for Chinese tourists. In addition, along with economic globalization, more and more tourism cooperation has broken through the boundaries among countries, fields, industries, and sectors. In China, tourism has become one of major ways of leisure for modern people. Rapidly increasing outbound tourism and popular FIT drive the growth in tourism consumption significantly, while UnionPay card is becoming a necessity for Chinese tourists, both at home and abroad, in other words, almost all Chinese tourists are UnionPay card holders. UnionPay is devoting itself to building cooperation platform between tourism and banking, to continuously better tourists' payment experience.

Secondly, the consumption behavior of Chinese outbound tourists shows two major features in 2014.

On the whole, the consumption behavior of Chinese outbound tourists in 2014 shows the following features: 1) bigger scale of consumption amount and higher transaction frequency; 2) more rational consumption behavior.

As the number of people involved in outbound tourism is increasing, the scale of outbound consumption is growing continuously. According to data published by CNTA, in 2014 the consumption of outbound tourism will exceed 115 billion U.S. dollars, equivalent to RMB 724.2 billion yuan, with a year-on-year growth rate of over

40%. Meanwhile, the consumption by card abroad also maintains fast growth. Due to enhanced network service capacity, UnionPay payment has become the first choice of Chinese outbound tourists. UnionPay's data about the first three quarters indicated that, Chinese tourists finished over 100 million transactions in foreign countries, and the growth rate in the number of transactions was twice as many as that in the amount of money of transactions. You can imagine that, in overseas market, every day more than one million outbound tourists consume by card, and such a great scale is enough to prove the image of China as a rising tourism power.

Along with the increase in the scale of consumption amount and frequency, tourists' consumption feature has changed as well. Their consumption channels are more diversified and consumption behavior is more rational. We find that, the range of overseas consumption becomes wider and wider, extending from simple shopping in the past to consumption in holiday, leisure, local experience, and others; particularly, UnionPay card is used more in places like department stores and supermarkets. Because in recent years UnionPay card has covered more and more stores of daily goods, and meanwhile Chinese tourists, different from single shopping in the past, more pursue travel quality and like to explore local culture.

Thirdly, tourists use UnionPay card in more destinations and for more purposes.

Chinese tourists also choose Europe, America, and Australia besides traditional destinations like Japan, Korea, and Southeast Asia. And in some popular emerging destinations, suppliers more actively support consumption by card to attract more Chinese young tourists, who are not large in number but present distinguishing features.

In traditional hot destinations, the safe environment of consumption by card and wider UnionPay card coverage further advance consumption of Chinese outbound tourists. Take South Korean market as an example, this year because President XI

Jinping visited South Korea, Sino-Korea relations enter a new stage, and there is no doubt that Korean businessmen are the biggest beneficiaries. In 2014, thanks to South Korean convenient payment environment for UnionPay card, Chinese tourists spend much more money there. In shopping areas like Myeongdong and Dongdaemun, Chinese tourists can pay directly by UnionPay card. Moreover, there are also words of greeting and information about discount written in Chinese, which facilitate the shopping experience of Chinese tourists in South Korea.

Other emerging overseas destinations, including Greece, Austria, Turkey, New Zealand, etc, are attracting more and more Chinese tourists. In these regions, Chinese tourists particularly like to experience local lifestyle, and they mostly spend money in food and beverage and tourist sites.

Influenced by the films of The Hobbit and Babaqunar 2 (Daddy, where are we going), far more Chinese tourists go to New Zealand. The type of tourism has been changing from short-term shopping tour with low value to FIT tour with relatively long stay. FIT tourists will promote the increase in consumption in New Zealand tourism market. Now it is very convenient for Chinese tourists to use UnionPay card in hot cities and towns like Auckland, Rotorua, and Queenstown. What's more, Chinese tourists also spend much more money in favorite scenic spots like grange, culture village, and hot spring.

Fourthly, UnionPay International commits itself to Chinese outbound tourists.

During the last decade, the number of overseas service suppliers accepting UnionPay card increased from 123 thousand in 2004 to over 13 million in 2014, with a growth rate of more than 1,000. In 2004 the volume of trade was only several billions, but today's annual compound growth rate reaches nearly 80%. So we can conclude that, the network expansion and service capacity of UnionPay card are directly proportional to both the number of Chinese outbound tourists and its growth rate.

To let UnionPay card holders benefit more, UnionPay International has prepared many preferential options for outbound tourists. In 2014, UnionPay International launches marketing campaigns in global 60 large airports, 40 well-known business districts, and 30 tourist attractions, richening the preferential plan for card holders. The 60 airports cover global top five duty-free groups, and include 18 of top 20 international passenger traffic airports. With regard to the activities in the 40 well-known business districts, most suppliers discount 10 percent for UnionPay card payment, while over one thousand suppliers offer exclusive discount. Next week we will start up more wonderful marketing campaigns in the 30 tourist attractions, welcome tourism fellows and UnionPay card holders to share together.

In the meanwhile, UnionPay is enjoying a better reputation in international market. In early December you will see UnionPay at the Mnet Asian Music Awards (MAMA) in Hong Kong. Furthermore, the UnionPay brand also presents its charm to the world on a lot of occasions, for instance, at the water fountain performance in Sentosa, Singapore; during leisure and entertainment in Asiatique, Bangkok, Thailand; at the lighting ceremony of Champs-Elysees Avenue in Paris, France; in the collection brochure of the British Museum, and so on.

In the short run we will cooperate with UNWTO on tourism consumption research, optimization of tourism payment, brand cooperation and promotion, etc. In addition, we and CTA will jointly conduct thorough analysis on the consumption behavior of Chinese outbound tourists, and release Report on Consumption of Chinese Outbound Tourists together in the near future.

Once again, many thanks go to CNTA and UNWTO! Wish this forum all success! Thank you very much!

Session 3
Panel Discussion

Panel Speech 1
China's Inbound Tourism Session: How to Promote Sustainable Growth of China's Inbound Tourism

Moderated by Prof. YANG Weiwu, Secretary of the Shanghai Institute of Tourism Committee

(November 14, 2014, Shanghai, P. R. China)

Moderator:

Dear friends, good afternoon!

I am YANG Weiwu, from Shanghai Institute of Tourism. Next, I will moderate the panel discussion on China inbound tourism. In this session, the first topic is "China Inbound Tourism Session: How to Promote Sustainable Growth of China's Inbound Tourism".

Today, along with the explosive increase in the amount of information, tourists' interest has changed rapidly, so traditional ways of marketing are far from meeting the requirements of market development. More and more countries and destinations make great efforts to improve marketing effect of inbound tourism via new media like Internet, mobile phone, and blog.

I now pass the floor to Mr. LI Hong, Director-General of Hangzhou Tourism Commission. Hangzhou is an excellent tourism city in China, and has achieved great success in media marketing. He will share their experiences with us. His speech topic is Media Marketing in the Internet Era. Mr. LI, the floor is yours!

Media Marketing in the Internet Era

Mr. Li Hong (Director-General of Hangzhou Tourism)

(November 14, 2014, Shanghai, P. R. China)

Honorable leaders, friends, ladies, and gentlemen,

Good afternoon! Thanks all the organizers for giving me this opportunity to share with you some information and thoughts on media marketing for outbound market by Hangzhou tourism Commission (HTC).

I. New situation, new trend

According to statistics, in 2013, the number of global inbound tourists totaled 1.087 billion, an annual growth of 5%; China received 129.0778 million inbound tourists, witnessing an annual decrease of 2.51%, while the number of overnight guests reached 55.6859 million, seeing an annual decrease of 3.53%. The growth of the number of inbound tourists fell from 7.91% (average) during 2001 to 2005 to 2.21% (average) during 2006 to 2010, 1.24% in 2011, and -2.23% in 2012. Different from rapidly increasing domestic tourism and outbound tourism, inbound tourism market is affected by various factors at home and abroad, and suffers great pressure from the decreasing trend. After long-term high-speed development, China's inbound tourism is gradually entering a normalized growth stage.

Facing new situation, we shall rationally analyze market, have crisis awareness, and meanwhile be confident in ourselves. As to the promotion of inbound tourism, our current tasks are to respond to need and change, develop new marketing idea, rely on technology, promote the intelligent integration of new media and event marketing.

II. Theoretical support for government tourism marketing in the Internet era

We understand that, main contents and purposes of government tourist destination marketing in the Internet era are to, on the basis of new technologies like (mobile) Internet, cloud computing, GPS, big data, and artificial intelligence, collect, manage, and analyze audience behavior and marketing effect, so as to direct tourism enterprises or help them to build public resource platform, integrate on-line and off-line marketing recourses, better marketing tactics and action execution, and realize the integration of precision marketing and effectiveness marketing in tourism.

On-line marketing and off-line marketing depend on different types of media, namely "new media and traditional media". Traditional media possesses content advantage while new media channel advantage. The current problem is that, traditional media are involved in the channel of new media, while new media also emphasize content, so it seems that content combines with channel and new media combine with traditional media. Actually, traditional media and new media, however, own different strengths in content and channel, such situation can be called "division of labor" and "cooperation", or even "Coopetition". Along with the development of digital and network technologies, audience differentiation (different customers favor different media forms and different contents), and different information consumption demand in different contexts, only by integration can traditional media and new media meet needs of different clients.

The integration of traditional media and new media is also essential to integrated marketing communication (IMC). The IMC theory, which was put forward in the

1990s by Prof. Don Schultz specializing in marketing in American Northwestern University, refers to the process of integrating all communication activities related to marketing. IMC, on the one hand, includes all communication activities such as advertisement, sales promotion, public relations (PR), and direct sale among marketing activities, and on the other hand, is able to communicate the integrated information to the audience. Its essence is to take meeting need of audience by communicating with them as value orientation, determine unified promotion tactics, coordinate and employ different media methods, make full use of different media, and thus reach a promotion peak with the best price/performance ratio.

III. Practice of HTC in innovative tourism marketing and promotion

HTC entrusted PATA with research on inbound market of main countries in Europe and America in 2009, and launched integrated marketing of traditional media in 2010. In recent years, based on this, HTC has perfected the IMC theory in the light of the development trend of media, introduced new media in an all-round manner, and applied it into marketing and promotion of inbound tourism market. At the end of 2012, HTC was actively engaged in intelligent tourism marketing, planned the global recruitment of "Contemporary Marco Polo-Doctor of Hangzhou" and a series of marketing projects themed by "Marco Polo". The campaign started in March 2013 and is still in progress now.

(I) Lay solid foundations

During innovating on marketing and promotion of city tourism, HTC has established a project group, to gather together experts, scholars, We Media, and enterprises to make thorough researches into such theories as integrated marketing and features of new media tools, and survey the use habits of overseas new media, correlation between tourism consumption and new media, and other issues.

Under the guidance of the IMC theory, after deeply researching and fully understanding characteristics of new media, HTC has developed new marketing and promotion plans, precisely established the support system of marketing and promotion for tourism, correctly found the best platform for new media marketing, meticulously designed the theme originality of "Marco Polo", accurately implemented a series of activities with "Hangzhou gene", and sincerely maintained relations with fans on social media.

(II) Event planning

"Event marketing" is a very effective measure to attract public attention. But the activity of "Look for Contemporary Marco Polo-Doctor of Hangzhou" shows a different way of event marketing: it doesn't just stand out for a short while, but lasts for a long time and contains numerous contents. During the two-year marketing and promotion project of "Marco Polo", the single theme lasts from beginning to end, the five phases advance one by one, and the four Internet experience activities link with each other.

From the beginning of selection, HTC actually has created an atmosphere of event marketing, connecting Hangzhou's cultural elements with on-line interaction experience, providing overseas Internet users with interactive virtual experience, making them know this city, obtaining exclusive "Hangzhou impression", and implanting the brand and value of city tourism in the audience's minds imperceptibly.

(III) Integration of media

The "Hangzhou impression" promotion campaign mainly relies on the top four popular social media in the English world, namely Facebook, Twitter, Pinterest, and YouTube. The four platforms are placed different emphases on. And due to their attributes of social contact, Hangzhou tourism is able to change from "concentrated broadcast" in the past to "point-to-point live broadcast", and by this way marketing is facing each independent person with the ability to re-communicate information.

In the meanwhile, the project, on the strength of on-line/off-line, domestic/foreign, and official/civil media and PR, takes "Look for Marco Polo" as the focus of event marketing, and forms a good situation of interaction between traditional media and new media and between domestic platform and foreign platform.

(IV) Emphasize the realization

During the implementation of the marketing and promotion project themed by "Marco Polo", as to the four overseas mew media platforms, HTC starts from scratch, constantly gropes, firstly ensures that all dominant indicators like the number of fans are accomplished, then pursues such indicators as interaction rate and conversion rate that can more reflect account activity and relations between fans, particularly pays much attention to how to combine innovative promotion and innovative marketing, and accomplishes the realization of potential market via tourism e-commerce, so as to bring tourism enterprises with new tourist source.

To promote on-line activities, HTC puts a certain number of advertisements on Internet, placing various static advertisements on roughly 20 mainstream tourism websites in Europe and America by the form of Internet alliance. We take advantage of advanced technologies, like the semantic analysis of Internet and IP direction, to realize exact advertising and thus win the maximum promotion effect with the minimum investment.

At the same time, HTC focuses on the two necessary factors of inbound tourism—"plane ticket + hotel", popularizes the "Marco Polo" campaign in foreign famous B2B companies, and establishes on-line booking channel, so that each European and American tourist who has interest in Hangzhou can reserve Hangzhou tourism products conveniently and cheaply.

IV. Outcomes of innovative tourism marketing and promotion by HTC

The marketing and promotion project themed by "Marco Polo" indicates that marketing and promotion of Hangzhou tourism has entered the new media era, and also brings significant results to Hangzhou tourism.

(I) Attract overseas Hangzhou fans

The marketing and promotion project themed by "Marco Polo" depends on the combination of overseas promotion and domestic experience, combines the communication ways of Internet new media with the overseas spread of brand image better, and thus increases the number of fans and improves their activity.

By October 2014, the official account of Hangzhou tourism possessed 58,583 Facebook fans, 4,932 Twitter fans, and 1,599 Pinterest fans, and there were 25,924 people taking part in "Contemporary Marco Polo" (the deadline was May 2014). And the number of interaction on Facebook averages over 100, and about 3,000 people participate in interaction monthly on average. Also many Chinese cities have opened official account of tourism on overseas social media platforms, Hangzhou tourism has the largest number of platforms and fans and among them European and American take a relatively large proportion, which effectively improves the reputation of the brand of Hangzhou tourism among targeted Internet users, especially among European and American people.

(II) Overcome difficulties in the realization of marketing

Government tourism marketing and promotion always faces the difficult problem of how to accomplish the realization of potential market. During the implementation of the marketing and promotion project themed by "Marco Polo", HTC focuses on the two essential factors of inbound tourism—"plane ticket + hotel", and cooperates with some foreign famous B2B company in popularizing the "Marco Polo" campaign, ensuring that each European or American tourist who is interested in Hangzhou can reserve hotel and plane ticket conveniently and cheaply, and improving the conversion rate of marketing and promotion.

Data provided by this B2B company showed that, only within two months, the booking rate of hotels in Hangzhou saw a year-on-year growth of 15%, much higher than the national level of 7%, and the reservation rate of some hotel in Hangzhou even witnessed a year-on-year growth of 139%. Thanks to this B2B platform, fans of facebook account of Hangzhou tourism increased by 7,000 in the same period of time, while both social media and tourism reservation grew significantly. Obviously, Hangzhou tourism has made an effective innovation in marketing and promotion, and such attempt has become a new power to drive new economy of Hangzhou tourism.

(III) Gain international reputation

On October 10, during the Marketing Events Awards 2014 organized by the internationally authoritative magazine Marketing in Sentosa, Singapore, the global recruitment of "Contemporary Marco Polo-Doctor of Hangzhou" planned and executed by HTC won the silver award of Best Government Sector Event (event marketing) over more than 400 counterparts, including United Nations Fund. The golden award was earned by 2013 International Fleet Review of Royal Australian Navy. The "Marco Polo" program also ranked among top five Best Use of Social Media. This prize is an internationally authoritative barometer of excellent advertising performance, and is the only one selected completely by customer marketing personnel.

(IV) Obtain super-value PR benefit

European and American media, like Forbes, NBC, The Guardian, The Daily Telegraph, Le Figaro, Conde Nast Traveller (global leading tourism magazine), and Yahoo US, and domestic media, like Xinhua News Agency, People's Daily, CCTV, Sina, and Tencent, all pay great attention to the "Marco Polo" campaign, and have made a lot of news reports on it. Because of these reports, some foreign media even actively search Hangzhou tourism, and report it more deeply, such as US Today.

According to HTC's survey in earlier stage and experience in media & PR, the whole page of American mainstream newspaper is priced at RMB 300,000 to 500,000 yuan (not including cost of writing advertorial), so the marketing and promotion project themed by "Marco Polo" has at least earned Hangzhou a overseas PR value of RMB 50 million yuan. The article themed by "How can Hangzhou promote tourism with a 55,000-dollar competition" on the Linkedin website said that, "It is a little early to talk about ROI. But because of this Hangzhou attracts the attention of traditional media and new media, It's certainly worth it."

V. Share experience

HTC has accumulated some experience and thoughts on IMC, targeted advertising placement on Internet, and tourism marketing and promotion through media integration (e.g. in MicroBlog, WeChat operation projects).

(I) Break advertisement limitation, foster communication idea.

It seems that the concepts of advertisement and communication have similar meaning, but there are actually great differences between the two. The action subject of advertisement is advertiser himself, and advertisement is a one-way communication mode of "I speak then you listen", and is subjective obviously; the action subject of advertisement, however, is the mass media, and communication appears to the public in the form of social media, is objective, and is a multi-way communication mode of "you speak, he speaks, and every one speaks", in addition, it strikes a balance between contents, focuses on topics the audience care about, emphasizes objectivity, and hides its advertising purpose and spreads it imperceptibly.

(II) Keep pace with technological progress, increase the type of platforms.

Twitter, Facebook, Pinterest, and Instragram (the latter two focus on vision share) are at the peak of development, while Blog, with a 16-year history, seems to be forgotten gradually. In China, when Sina and Tencent Microblog were very popular, WeChat was still unknown to the public. But only one year later, today WeChat has possessed the same number of users as Microblog. Along with the high-speed development of new media technologies and changing new media platforms, each platform is essential to tourism promotion and communication of destination. The more platforms we have, the more audience we can reach.

(III) Flexibly employ platform, introduce market mechanism.

The increase in the number of platforms brings about manpower and cost problems, therefore we choose platform flexibly, and emphasize resource integration, effectively solving these problems. We depend on ourselves to build website, Microblog, and WeChat platforms, and meanwhile buy public services from market, outsourcing part of new media platforms, especially those overseas business. Through contract restriction and KPI evaluation on service companies, we control the leading direction of promotion, and introduce market competition and vitality. We not only integrate advertisement into communication, but also improve market sensitivity, closely following the changes in technology and market.

(IV) Integrate on-line and off-line, combine different platform.

As to the comprehensive integration of on-line and off-line, only destinations that provide the fittest content at the fittest time and via the fittest channel can stand out. When tourism administrations in many foreign metropolises invest lots of resources and energy in building on-line social network platform, they still print tourism brochures as well. Any media platform has its limitation, so does new media platform. To cover all age groups, new media must cooperate with traditional media. In the meanwhile, different new media platforms target different customers, for instance, 80% of the audience of Pinterest, one of overseas new media platforms of Hangzhou tourism, are European and American women. In China, some companies in the FMCG (fast-moving consumer goods) Industry, in the light of different advantages of Microblog and WeChat, attract a large number of customers via Microblog and a small number of potential customers via WeChat. Their experience is also suitable for new media promotion of tourist destination.

Media marketing in the Internet era is a dynamic and constantly innovative evolution process, and HTC has just finished some preliminary exploration. It is my honor to share with you our experience. Thank you!

Moderator:

Thanks Li's wonderful remarks! He presented distinct opinions within such a short time.

Moderator:

Now let's welcome Ms. yu Ningning, Chairman of the Board, China International Travel Service Limited Head Office! She will share with us some experience in Development and Innovation of Tourism Products in the FIT Era! Ms. yu, the floor is yours!

Development and Innovation of Tourism Products in the FIT Era

Ms. Yu Ningning (Chairman of the Board, China International Travel Service Limited Head Office)

(November 14, 2014, Shanghai, P. R. China)

Honorable Mr. DU Jiang, Vice Chairman, China National Tourism Administration, leaders, ladies and gentlemen,

Good afternoon! It is my great honor to share with you development and innovation of inbound tourism products in the FIT era.

From 1978 to 2010, except in 1989 and 2003, China's inbound tourism always maintained sustained growth, which was essentially driven by "close-end bonus". In foreigners' eyes, China is always "traditional China", "mysterious country", "much different from the western world", which once stimulated foreign tourists to explore China and thus developed "China complex".

Nevertheless, since 2011, inbound tourism has always been in the doldrums, which is affected by many factors. Firstly, the economy of overseas markets remains generally in the doldrums, so their demand for long-haul tourism consumption reduces. Secondly, the rise of China makes western countries misunderstand it to some extent, and they negatively publicize China. Thirdly, in recent years, as inflation and booming outbound tourism cause competition for plane ticket, the product price of inbound tourism is on the high side, and exceeds the psychological expectation of foreign travelers. Fourthly, the products are updated slowly, at present most of inbound tourism products are still Beijing, Xi'an, Shanghai, Guangzhou, and the Three Gorges tour routes; moreover, because some tourist sites are excessively commercialized, the attraction of traditional original elements of inbound tourism weakens.

Although inbound tourism is in the doldrums, it still presents some new characteristics.

I: Tourism habit and tourism demand change. Along with the popularization of Internet and rising of mobile Internet, the proportions of group tour and FIT tour change, and FIT travelers segments grow. Annual Report of China Inbound Tourism Development 2014 released recently by CTA also reflects this feature.

II: China's tourism infrastructure is perfected day by day, network service covers throughout the country, the level of smart tourism improves, and the conditions of DIY tour and free tour are relatively mature.

III: "China charm" improves revisit rate.

Since its establishment in 1954, CITS has specialized in inbound tourism, witnessing the entire development course of China's inbound tourism. Despite inbound tourism market has developed slowly in recent years, CITS has always insisted on cultivating inbound tourism market, been ready to devote itself to the new state policy of vigorously developing inbound tourism, and actively explored the development and innovation of inbound tourism products in the FIT era.

Traditional ideas unduly oppose FIT tour again group tour. In fact, FIT is small group too, but FIT tourists just have more personal travel time and demand. The development and innovation of inbound tourism products shall focus on the following three aspects:

I. Innovate on the operation mode of inbound tourism, and strengthen the e-commerce construction of inbound tourism

Currently, inbound tourism products mostly depend on foreign wholesalers, and hence are passive in terms of R&D. if products can directly enter overseas consumption market, it will help develop and recommend new products, and reduce product cost. Of course, to directly enter foreign FIT market, we must invest more in earlier stage, in this regard, the state can formulate relevant policies to help develop and recommend FIT product. In accordance with overseas FIT market, we need to accelerate the construction of domestic reception infrastructure, and facilitate foreigners' reservation of hotel, plane ticket, and train ticket in China. In recent years, CITS has always taken the e-commerce development of inbound tourism as the major measure to reinforce inbound FIT market. It has established the e-commerce website of inbound tourism in multiple languages, and organized special department and special team to provide FIT tourists with tourism product, customized tourism, booking service of single product, and friendly website user experience, to supply tourists with detailed Chinese information to the greatest extent. Multi-language contents cover all tourism elements and develop relevant industries as much as possible, such as health preserving, hiking, cycling, mountaineering, and many volunteer activities. Such measure has obtained positive results.

II. Innovate on the product mode of inbound tourism, create "FIT group tour" product

At present, CITS actively develops "FIT group tour" product for FIT market, to adapt to different tour time and route of global tourists, re-arrange destination to provide differentiated services to meet common needs and individual needs of overseas tourists, increases route and destination of "FIT group tour", adds new sightseeing contents, and has obtained good effect. In the future, it will promote large-scale "FIT group tour".

III. Innovate on the content of inbound tourism product, and deeply explore the tourism connotation of tourist destination

On the one hand, expand fresh tourist destination. CITS strives to expand emerging destination besides well-known Beijing, Shanghai, Xi'an, and Guangzhou, such new destinations as the Silk Road, Grand Canal, Three Gorges, Tibet, and Southwest China, to cultivate new highlights in market.

On the other hand, develop the pith of Chinese tourism products, and explore the cultural connotation of products. As tourists have more and more travel experience, they present increasing demand for cultural experience. Besides typical tourist products like world cultural heritage, CITS will explore diversified cultural elements, such as food, music, history, religion, folk custom, landscape garden, and ancient town, to create richer cultural products. Meanwhile, on the strength of cultural tourism, vigorously develop in-depth tourism.

In short, we shall attract tourists to China through development and innovation of tourism products, and moreover attract tourists to revisit China, improving revisit rate and show more charm of "beautiful China". Thank you!

Moderator:

CITS is an outstanding travel agency in China, and our inbound tourism initially started from CITS.

Moderator:

Ms. yu just made a great analysis for us. Indeed, the structure of tourism market is changing, in the past we often said "attract tourists by the brand of travel agency and manage them by the flag in guide's hand", but nowadays the situation is completely different. Under current circumstances, what are the characteristics of China's inbound market?

Now let's welcome Ms. Katy Xu, Vcie President, Greater China and North Asia, BBC Worldwide. She will give BBC's Report On China's Inbound Tourism. Katy, the floor is yours!

BBC's Report On China's Inbound Tourism

Ms. Katy Xu (Vcie President, Greater China and North Asia, BBC Worldwide)

(November 14, 2014, Shanghai, P. R. China)

Honorable Mr. DU Jiang, Vice Chairman, and dear friends,

Good afternoon! It's indeed a great pleasure to be here with you, and this is the third time that BBC contributes to CNTA's symposium. In the video, you could see BBC's development in recent years and our reports on China's tourism. Every year, according to BBC's statistics on the latest global survey data, we make some suggestions for China's inbound tourism. Today, we are here for the same purpose.

Previous speakers have mentioned that China's inbound tourism has developed slowly in the past several years. The growth rate is slow, but foreign tourists traveling to China are wealthy, they annually spend 70 billion U.S dollars in their vacation in China, and 63% of the expenditure has nothing to do with traffic. One fourth of BBC's audience said they expended 2,500 U.S dollars or above on the last tour, equivalent to RMB 15,000 yuan. Although they don't come to China frequently, every time their actual consumption and its driving force for China's GDP growth are huge.

The reason why China's inbound tourism develops slowly is also because neighboring countries and regions put great efforts into international marketing. Mainland China is faced with competitors like Thailand, Malaysia, Hong Kong,

Macao, and emerging Vietnam. We all see that, these countries regions vigorously advertise their culture, city, or even entire country via foreign media.

Here, I'd like to discuss why the audience of international news is essential to China's inbound tourism.

Firstly, this part of audience are not only leisure tourists, but also high-end business travelers and decision-makers of MICE. For example, 41% of BBC's audience are commercial decision-makers, who are able to determine the next conference place for their companies more easily. Meanwhile, they are also opinion leaders, and 78% of them usually tell their family and friends information about new products and services, so if you can affect this group of people, your marketing work will produce ripple effect. In addition, we acquire a group of very interesting data: 75% of well-off European tourists don't adopt the plan of travel plan, and plan their outbound tourism by themselves. With regard to these tourists, you can conduct direct, face-to-face marketing, or tell them information via Internet, so that they are able to directly make plans for commercial purchase and tour on Internet.

Most of BBC's audience are China addicts. Take the audience in Asia & Pacific for example, 72% of users come to China for the commercial purpose, while 55% for leisure. In Europe, in 2013, 1.3 million users visited China, and in America the number was 2.1 million. These audience pay much attention to China and Asia, so we shall further influence them to visit China once again, twice again…

I often have to answer the question: how long does it take foreign tourists to design their tour? In general, the time is directly proportional to their distance from China, and 30% of European and American travelers would plan their long-haul tour three to six months earlier. In Asia, due to shorter distance, tourists often make their travel plan one to two months in advance; if there are some weekend tourism packages or holiday packages, maybe more such people will visit China.

When to start out? This is another problem people always care about. Summer is still the peak period of American and European tourists, while the audience in Asia &Pacific prefer to travel to China in winter.

The audience of international news could be influenced at all times, since they use more than one medium, just as previous speakers mentioned, in 24 hours, except sleeping time, they are differently affected by different media, when they make tour plan, different platforms also play a different role in their decision making. For instance, the audience of international news may be stimulated to travel when watching TV, and then they use digital media to conduct specific survey and reserve tour package on Internet. Whether during commercial tour or leisure tourism they try to keep in touch with news media; during holidaying 92% of the audience get to know international news anytime, anywhere, and keep in contact with their friends and family. On holiday, they don't like to bother about work, and only 9% of tourists want to know information about work.

In summary, the audience of news reported by international media, during the whole tourism decision-making, stay in close contact with international media. Destinations can take this golden opportunity to affect them. A lot of tourists think BBC's tourism programs and contents of tourism website are highly believable and attractive. When choosing tourist destinations, they would like to make reference to BBC tourism. BBC's travel show is a reliable flagship program, and as you just saw in the video, we have made numerous reports on China's tourist sites, including new ones, old ones, and little-known ones. In 2014, part of the Great Wall of China got a designated graffiti area, on which we conducted an interesting report; in the meanwhile, we deeply reported Sanya's sunshine, beach, as well as forest and national park. In the Internet era, the www.bbc.com/Travel channel is a digital platform inspiring many audience to travel. In 2014, we reported the Silk Road, Hainan-

China's paradise of exiles, and Beijing's extraordinary Grand Canal. As the audience of international news have little spare time and work at high pressure, they hope to know unknown information about familiar destinations, and appreciate beautiful photos and exquisite tourism stories. Even when surfing the Internet, they want to find some desired information quickly and easily. Moreover, they also expect to learn about a few unknown destinations. We must take their curiosity into consideration in the process of destination marketing. 75% of the audience think that, "when I am on holiday, the most important thing for me is to experience local culture". On the world news station, BBC has largely advertised and reported China's many tourism bases, including report on 72-hour transit visa exemption, and originally advertising tourism administrations in Beijing, Sanya, and many other provinces and cities. We possess 380 million TV users and 76 million Internet users throughout the world, who trust BBC very much, so all information about little-known destinations or well-known ones released on this platform will greatly influence their decision on tourism subscription.

Before I finish my speech, I want to give leaders in charge of destination marketing three suggestions.

First, the audience of international news are both leisure tourists and commercial tourists, so when communicating information we must combine these two factors, to kill two birds with one stone;

Second, the audience of international news are affected by various media, and TV and digital mobile media have different impact on them at different time;

Third, the audience of international news are not very sensitive to price, but they prefer little-known, picturesque and very spiritual places, from which they can also get inspiration. When making plans for destination marketing we shall make more efforts to attract such high-end, well-off clients, BBC is willing to cooperate with more tourism administrations in China, and give you advice and suggestions.

Thank you!

Moderator:

Many thanks for Katy's brilliant speeches! Now let's go on to the panel session.

Panel Discussion 1 Discussion on How to Maintain Sustainable Growth of China's Inbound Tourism and the Promotion

Moderated by Prof. YANG Weiwu, Secretary of the Shanghai

Institute of Tourism Committee

(November 14, 2014, Shanghai, China)

Moderator:

In this session, we would like to welcome four honorable guests, they are:

Mr. Tsou Hsin Chiang, Vice Chairman of South Korea Association of Travel Agents, Honarary Vice Mayor of Seoul, President of Simon King Travel Co., Ltd

Mr. Markus Walter, General Manager of Diamir Erlebnisreisen GmbH

Mr. Vikas Khanduri, CEO, Holiday Merchants

Mr. Ross Jackson, Vice President, Asia and Pacific, VISA

Please take a seat, each speaker.

The four speakers come from different countries, and care about China's tourism all the time. As you are engaged in different industries, I hope Mr. Tsou Hsin Chiang, Mr. Markus Walter, and Mr. Vikas Khanduri could give your opinions about the following themes,

1. From point of view of travel agencies, what barriers to China inbound tourism shall we break through currently;

2. From tourists' point of view, what do tourists in your country think of China;

3. From tourist's point of view, what dominant factors cause the decrease in tourist satisfaction;

4. In terms of market feature, what basic behavior or law characteristics do tourists have;

5. At present and in the next period of time, what expectations do tourism enterprises in your country, especially travel agencies, have for China.

Since Mr. Ross Jackson is from famous VISA, I suggest Mr. Ross Jackson give us some opinions from the following aspects,

1. What do main tourist source markets think of China's inbound tourism;

2. Basic condition of consumption of card in China's inbound tourism;

3. Current barriers of consumption of card in China's inbound tourism;

4. Successful cases of promoting consumption of card in inbound tourism by overseas developed tourist destinations;

5. Relevant measures VISA has taken to accelerate the internationalization of China's inbound tourism and facilitate consumption of card, as well as successful experience.

As we don't have much time, each speaker will express your opinions within eight minutes. Now, our first speaker is Mr. Tsou Hsin Chiang.

Marketing Plan for Sustainable Development of China's Inbound Tourism

Mr. Tsou Hsin Chiang (Vice Chairman of Korea Association of Travel Agents, Honarary Vice Mayor of Seoul, President of Simon King Travel Co., Ltd)

(November 14, 2014, Shanghai, P. R. China)

Ladies and gentlemen,

Good afternoon! I am Tsou Hsin Chiang, Vice Chairman of Korea Association of Travel Agents. I'd like to take the successful marketing case of Zhangjiajie tourism product in Korea for example to elaborate on marketing plan for sustainable development of China's inbound tourism.

Since its first development in South Korea in 2005, except in 2009 when South Korea suffered financial crisis, Zhangjiajie tourism product has grown continuously. South Korean travel agencies and companies regard people aged 40 to 60 as the major consumption group of Zhangjiajie tourism product, and employ the following plans to advertise it:

I. Place advertising screens at metro interchange stations, and post up advertisements in airports or in buses;

II. Use LED screens to play advertising videos in busy business areas and crowded areas;

III. Collect information about Zhangjiajie tourism, and print it on magazines, posters, brochures, handbills, etc, and distribute them in targeted market.

To continuously carry out successful cases like Zhangjiajie, South Korean travel agencies and companies, under the support of China's central government and local governments, actively explore new tourist destinations, develop products suitable for features of new tourist sites, and popularize them in many ways. It's important to note that, while advertising in South Korea, the Chinese party also needs to place in tourist sites Korean signs, which must be expressed accurately and can be understood by Korean travelers; at present, many Korean signs, due to unclear meaning, fail to meet with expected results.

To maintain the sustainable development of inbound tourism market, we must ensure tourists will come back in the future. To fully interpret the distinguishing features of scenic spots and realize safe tourism, the Chinese party needs to print diversified guidebooks in Korean. And further, hold communication meetings of tourism personnel and travel agencies of the two countries. For example, the cooperation and exchange symposium on the improvement of Sino-Korean tourism quality, which took place in Korean in August of this year, shall be convened again next year.

To attract more South Korean tourists to China, China shall implement the "visa upon arrival" system, and promote the visa exemption system.

Thanks for your attention! Thank you very much!

Moderator:

Thank you, Mr. Tsou Hsin Chiang! South Korea is China's number one tourist source, in this regard, South Korea Association of Travel Agents has done a lot of work, and indeed we see many South Korean tourists in Zhangjiajie.

Moderator:

Next, Let's welcome Mr. Jackson!

Quality Improvement of China's Inbound Tourism Market by Promoting Consumption of VISA Card

Mr. Ross Jackson (Vice President, Asia and Pacific, VISA)

(November 14, 2014, Shanghai, P. R. China)

From our point of view as VISA, we look at how many people travel and how much they spend, according to travel report we do every year, what we are seeing is that the spending is not up to the global average, as we discovered, travelers bring with them cash, and certainly limit their spend. For those you have to classify the affluence, for Chinese market, the spend is high, but they still carry themselves with cash.

In a recent survey, we see that the top three cities that attract most tourists, cash withdraw is growing. Because as the infrastructure is improving especially in the second tier cities. According to the case study, we'd like to point out the cash really help travelers to enjoy the local food, to enjoy the attractions of the culture, to easily move around with transportation. The key category is dining in China, the result shows that spend will increase if the card acceptance is wider in restaurants and other casual places. The other area that we look at is what can be done in the source market. If we take the case study as example, how we support that, from long-haul markets, we often look at the promotion the ability to get cash when you wanted in China and source market like Russia. We also promote key segments in other markets such as the ease of spending. You know, I think there is more to be done. We are now focusing on some key categories in some major cities and its sub-regions. We use a lot media, traditional or non-traditional, we really focus on source market to promote it. From our point of view, from the industry's point of view, there are a lot of opportunities to cooperate in tourism sector. We are not really drive the number of tourists, but to maximize the value for tourists. Thank you!

Moderator:

Thank you, Mr. Jackson! Mr. Jackson, from the angle of consumption of VISA card, analyzed the reasons for the growth of consumption of card and problems caused by the growth, thereby analyzing behavior of China's inbound tourists.

Moderator:

Germany is China's largest source market in Western European. Next, let's welcome Mr. Markus Walter, General Manager of Diamir Erlebnisreisen GmbH.

Changes of German Tourists' Demands in FIT Era

Mr. Markus Walter (General Manager of Diamir Erlebnisreisen GmbH)

(November 14, 2014, Shanghai, P. R. China)

Thank you for inviting me to share our experiences with you. We are a tour operator, specialized on small group and FIT tours worldwide. China is not all our business but very important part.

We have been offering tours to China for 15 years, but things have changed a lot. As the society develops, tourists are quite different from those 20 years ago. The general recognition of China as a tourist destination, for German tourists, China is beautiful with landscape, great cultural heritage, it happens to be influenced by media coverage, worldwide international media. From our German point of view, it is really a great challenge for tourism advertisements to get the media coverage in their sense, even during the Olympic Games in Beijing, a lot of media in Germany were still reporting pollution, scandals more than sports or beautiful scenes of the country, it is still the similar situation. There is a lot politics in media.

The challenge for tourism industry is to establish China as a safe and modern destination in the minds of tourists. There is one thing stayed the same as many years ago is language use, because even in big city like Beijing or Shanghai, it's still very hard to have a nice talk with taxi driver or waiters in the restaurants. I hope very much this will change in the next few years.

The satisfaction index of German tourist to China decreased, not because of the destination, but because the advance demands increased, a lot of development of our life happened, basic requirements like transportation or lodging are much more higher than 10 years ago.

Many German who came to China used to be between 45 to 60 years old, that changed a lot.

Today a great variety of people come to China and group tours have been main stream for many years, now FIT to China is completely another type of tourism and requests very different infrastructure.

My wish as a tour operator, we could improve the circumstances for tourists, starting visa facilitation for instance. When I traveled to China for the very first time 14 years ago, I spent 30 Euros and filled in one page visa application form, now this time I spent 100 Euros and four pages of application, that's increased 300-400% just for getting the visa. I don't think this helps to get more tourists. So visa convenience is essential. Thank you!

Moderator:

Thank you, Mr. Markus Walter!

Moderator:

Next, let's welcome Mr. Vikas Khanduri, CEO, Holiday Merchants. His seat is most distant from me, but actually our two countries adjoin.

After Mr. Khanduri finished his remarks, I want to invite each speaker to give a word of suggestion for China's inbound tourism.

Let's welcome Mr. Khanduri!

Preferences of Indian Tourists and Barriers of India-China Tourism Market

Mr. Vikas Khanduri (CEO, Holiday Merchants)

(November 14, 2014, Shanghai, P. R. China)

I'm from New deli. I think we are closest to China, and there is big potential for our tourism cooperation. I also feel the Chinese tourism office is doing a lot in India. For example, they've created English website, I think that helps a lot. The problem is connectivity. I also agree that visa is a difficulty. Although it should not be a hard process, it impresses it is so. Because the connectivity is low, that's why it very difficult to organize for tour operator.

Indians are keen on food, some travelers might say proudly when they come back from the trip: I have traveled to China, I made food in a certain restaurants. This is something needs to be done. 2015 will a dynamic year for China and India. It gives an indicator that destination planning to be done, I see the MICE tours will increase a lot.

We do need more knowledge about China, not only about Beijing, Shanghai, but also some other parts of China. Thank you!

Moderator:

Thank you, Mr. Vikas Khanduri! We also sincerely hope India-China Tourism become better and better.

As what I said a moment ago, let's welcome each speaker to give a word of suggestion for China's inbound tourism.

Tsou Hsin Chiang, Vice Chairman of South Korea Association of Travel Agents, Honarary Vice Mayor of Seoul, President of Simon King Travel Co., Ltd

I'd like to take this opportunity to thank CNTA for inviting me to attend this symposium! Tourism market is enormous, and we must face success and failure calmly. Correct errors, if any. We aren't afraid of problems, but the worst thing is that we refuse to solve them. I wish China's inbound tourism all success! Thank you!

Mr. Ross Jackson, Vice President, Asia and Pacific, VISA

We all need to put our customers at first and from VISA point of view, we have 2 billion card holders, we are trying to remove the barriers for visitors to pay here in China. I think there are key ways to maximize the value of the tourists who are coming here, the easy way to pay that is used worldwide is my suggestion. Thank you!

Mr. Markus Walter, General Manager of Diamir Erlebnisreisen GmbH

From my perspective, our main target is to get tourists involved, and not just to have them watching, because once the trip became their life experiences, they might come back in the future. That's why I really like to let tourists in, don't separate them into different restaurants, hotels, or certain areas only for tourists but all parts of the society. This way is far more sustainable. Thank you!

Mr. Vikas Khanduri , CEO, Holiday Merchants

I think, Indians are known for their shopping anywhere they go. They go to Switzerland, they buy 20kg of chocolate. As Indians, I think you are shopping focused as well. So shopping convenience is quite important.

Moderator:

These four speakers and the three speakers in the previous session showed us a wonderful feast of opinions and ideas. We realize that: to promote the sustainable growth of China's inbound tourism, the government shall formulate tourism-related policies in aspects of visa, tax, finance, banking, traffic rights, and transit service; tourism competent authorities at all levels shall strive to improve tourism image and advertise in overseas market; market entities and tourism enterprises shall make great efforts to innovate on inbound tourism products. Moreover, citizens and tourists shall work hand in hand in this regard. Only by common efforts can we better China's inbound tourism. Let's give a big hand to all speakers, and thanks for their wonderful remarks!

That's all for Panel 1 "China Inbound Tourism Session: How to Promote Sustainable Growth of China's Inbound Tourism?"

Next panel "China Outbound Tourism Session: How to Share the Opportunity of China's Outbound Tourism?" will be chaired by Mr. XU Jing, Director of Regional Programme for Asia and the Pacific, UNWTO. Once again, many thanks go to all speakers! I now pass the floor to Director XU Jing.

Panel Speech 2
China's Outbound Tourism Session: How to Share the Opportunity of China's Outbound Tourism

Moderated by Mr. XU Jing, Director of Regional Programme

for Asia and the Pacific, UNWTO

(November 14, 2014, Shanghai, P. R. China)

Moderator:

Ladies and gentlemen,

Good afternoon!

Next, let's start today's second panel. Although it is put at the end of the symposium, from UNWTO point of view, this part is the highlight. Outbound tourism, especially China's outbound tourism, is a hot potato. As everyone knows, the number of China's outbound tourists has been extremely huge, and in 2014 outbound tourists will reach 100 million. In the context of such a large number, how much do people in other countries know about needs of China's outbound tourists? Maybe you will tell me, foreigners know Chinese want to drink hot water, but anything else? Secondly, the reason we are assembled here to discuss China's outbound tourism is mainly because the number of over 100 million outbound tourists are beyond all expectations of UNWTO and all other institutes. In this context, today we will take more than one hour to listen to experts' explanation. Firstly, let's welcome Mr. LI Zhongguang, Director, Institute of Tourism Industry and Enterprise Development, China Tourism Academy. He will release Chinese Outbound Tourist Satisfaction Investigation Report. Mr. LI, the floor is yours!

2013 Chinese Outbound Tourist Satisfaction Investigation Report

Dr. LI Zhongguang (Director, Institute of Tourism Industry and Enterprise Development, China Tourism Academy)

(November 14, 2014, Shanghai, P. R. China)

Ladies and gentlemen:

It's my great pleasure to release this investigation report on behalf of the research group of "Chinese Outbound Tourist Satisfaction Investigation" of China Tourism Academy (CTA).

I. Overview

As everyone knows, in recent years the number of Chinese outbound tourists has been increasing sharply. To better meet the requirements of outbound tourists, resolve the problems related to market order of outbound tourism, promote international cooperation on tourism and provide firm survey foundations and effective priorities for international tourism development in the context of mass tourism, CTA, under the leadership of China National Tourism Administration, began to carry out a special survey of Chinese outbound tourist satisfaction in the first quarter of 2013. And the investigation aimed at 24 countries.

The same as the project of "National Tourist Satisfaction Investigation", which was developed earlier and had a larger scale, this investigation also belonged to foundation engineering of the destination evaluation system with tourists as the core established by China in recent years. We adopted the tourist satisfaction investigation system independently researched, developed and designed by CTA. This index system was established on the basis of the expectancy—perception theory, and fully absorbed tourists' numerous comments and opinions on the Internet. Its scientificity had been recognized by the international community, and in 2011 it received the "Award for Innovation in Government" given by the United Nations World Tourism Organization (UNWTO). In recent two years, we have interviewed over 30,000 tourists on the spot, collected more than one million vivid comments, and discovered tourists' comment result through detailed research. We have compiled, released and sent special reports for seven successive quarters.

The investigation result showed that Chinese outbound tourists were basically satisfied in general. During 2013-2014, satisfaction of Chinese outbound tourists was kept stably at the "basic satisfaction" level (more than 75) every quarter, and both the scores by tourists' interview on the spot or comment on the Internet reached over 75. Generally speaking, Chinese tourists' evaluation on foreign destinations was good. In recent two years, the average satisfaction indexes of foreign destinations' city image, city construction, city management, service of the public sector, and service of tourism were 81.90, 80.95, 80.12, 80.74 and 79.81 respectively, basically at the "satisfaction" level. However, in the meanwhile, satisfaction presented a slightly decline, mainly because the young group who preferred DIY tour gave lower score. According to feedback from tourists, their most expectations were the significant improvement of Chinese services and sense of security, and the effective promotion of tourism complaint satisfaction, for example, tourists frequently required Chinese travel guide, Chinese restaurant, Chinese TV program, Chinese website, Chinese housekeeping, China UnionPay, Alipay facilities, and other services.

II. Overview of Destination Countries

According to the survey, the 24 foreign destinations were divided into three groups. The first group was made up of the countries receiving the score of more than 80 at the "satisfaction" level, including Canada, New Zealand, Singapore, France, Britain and Australia. During the whole investigation, satisfaction of Singapore increased stably, and they ranked the top three for two successive quarters recently. Britain and France also adopted relevant policies and measures to sustainably improve tourists' experience, for example, Britain provided mobile visa service, and canceled group transit visa; France reduced the duration of applying for and approving visa, and increased police forces and Chinese restaurants in tourist sites.

The second group was made up of the countries receiving the score of 75 to 80 at the "basic satisfaction" level, including America, Spain, Italy, Japan, Germany, South Korea, Thailand, Argentina, South Africa, Malaysia, Russia, the Philippines, Brazil, Indonesia and Cambodia. Since the beginning of this year, satisfaction of Chinese travelling to Italy has increased significantly. This had something to do with the press conference on "Welcome Chinese" jointly promoted by the Italian government and CTA. The "Welcome Chinese" project developed by CTA is a standard service system "customized for Chinese tourists", aiming at close cooperation with operators of accommodations, food, stores, transportation, theme parks in destinations, helping foreign businessmen meet Chinese tourists' core appeals. Organizations such as Rome Airport and Nuovo Trasporto Viaggiatori (Italian: New Passenger Transport) obtained the "Welcome Chinese" certificate.

The third group was made up of the only three countries receiving the score of less than 75, including Vietnam, India and Mongolia. The analysis of tourists' comments showed that they were less satisfied with Chinese services, Chinese signs, sense of security and special culture, for example, in Mongolia tourists could feel absolutely nothing about its special culture atmosphere, and a lot of westernized characters totally replaced some of its traditional Mongolian characters.

In general, the score and ranking of satisfaction of the 24 sample countries were relatively stable. This was also closely related to those countries' comprehensive national power. We conducted an integrated analysis of the satisfaction score and per capita GDP, and found that countries with per capita GDP of 20,000 US dollars all received a average satisfaction score of higher than 78, including Canada, New Zealand, Singapore, France, Britain, Australia, America, Spain, Italy, Japan, Germany and South Korea; while those with lower per capita GDP received a lower score, including Argentina, South Africa, Malaysia, Russia, the Philippines, Brazil, Indonesia, Cambodia, Vietnam, India and Mongolia. However, Thailand surprised us, as it had relatively low per capita GDP but received a relatively high score, which indicated that Chinese tourists were much more satisfied with Thailand's tourism service than with other countries' comprehensive infrastructure.

III. Expectations and Suggestions

Since the implementation of the project of Chinese outbound tourist satisfaction investigation in 2013, CTA has conducted special research on outbound tourist satisfaction and ranked it, analyzed and studied market environment and public service of foreign countries' destination cities, over a long period of time systematically traced and analyzed main factors impacting tourist satisfaction, periodically released the survey result, so as to provide major destination cities with valuable Chinese experience for reference to promote their tourism quality. We established the system of periodical release through branch offices and mainstream media in destinations, sent satisfaction ranking and investigation report to destination countries' embassies and consulates, tourism promotion agencies, etc, and periodically organized domestic and foreign tourism authorities, tourism enterprises, tourism institutes, and other organizations to convene the workshop on Chinese outbound tourist satisfaction. We suggested to government departments, such as National Tourism Administration, the Ministry of Foreign Affairs and the Ministry of Commerce, and industrial organizations that they should consider the result of outbound tourist satisfaction as the key content during national foreign publicity and exchange. We also have established the consultation system of tourist satisfaction with destination countries and regions such as Singapore and Italy.

The increasing growth and healthy development of China's outbound tourism market is beneficial to both China and the world. As Chinese tourists require more about quality of service, we suggest the Chinese government and destination countries jointly striving to remove all policy barriers that harm people's free exchange, treat tourists well in every little part of reception, and try the best to guarantee security and quality, so as to supply tourists with satisfactory tourism experience environment. The government and tourism sector shall, based on the principle of mutual benefit, simplify visa procedures, reduce duration of processing visa application, cut down visa expenditure, and offer more other conveniences to outbound tourists. Bear in mind the interest of tourists in terms of language and consumption habit, provide more Chinese signs, Chinese media, Chinese guides and allow the utilization of China UnionPay in main distributing centers and destinations, and establish closer normalized cooperation systems in aspects of tourism standard, mutual recognition of qualifications for employment in tourism, early warning system of safety problems and disposal of emergent events. Include outbound tourism in the strategic planning of improving China's cultural soft power and promoting exchange and cooperation in the field of human culture, take outbound tourists as the carrier of state image to propagandize it more vividly, and bring the landing of Chinese satellite TV channels, easier import policies on Chinese books, more complete Chinese reception environment and other contents into the important conditions of opening up Chinese outbound tourism.

Moderator:

Many thanks, Director LI, for your official analysis report! I hope CTA will cooperate with UNWTO's Marketing Department, to share this tourist satisfaction report with tourist destinations all over the world, especially those engaged in China's outbound market.

Moderator:

Next, let's welcome Dr. WANG Xinjun , CEO of IVY Alliance Tourism Consulting. IVY Alliance is a Chinese consulting group specializing in outbound tourism.

Mr. WANG, the floor is yours!

China's Outbound Tourism Analysis—Market Structure and Trend

Mr. WANG Xinjun (CEO of IVY Alliance Tourism Consulting)

(November 14, 2014, Shanghai, P. R. China)

Honorable leaders, friends, ladies and gentlemen,

Good afternoon! It is a great pleasure to share with you our analysis of China's outbound tourism market.

Over the past decade, China's outbound tourism, from start-up to high-speed growth, has reflected the development of society and economy to some extent. Through years' development, outbound travel has become a lifestyle of more and more Chinese tourists. If we say the past decade was the golden decade of the rapid development of China's outbound tourism market, according to comprehensive evaluation on factors affecting outbound tourism, the next decade will be the decade of golden development, and the transformation and upgrading Version 2.0 of China's outbound tourism market.

Firstly, let's look at tourist flow structure of China's outbound tourism. By estimate, in 2014 China's outbound tourists will reach 110 million, 70% of them went to Hong Kong and Macao and 30% to the other destinations. Among tourist flow to third-country destinations, 69% traveled to Asia, while 31% to long-haul destinations like Europe, America, Oceania, and Africa.

Next, let's pass on to tourist source structure of China's outbound tourism. China possesses a very large territory, and the economic level varies with regions. According to GDP per capita of cities' and towns' population, and number of middle-class and well-off families, we divide China's outbound source market into first-tier, second-tier, and third-tier markets. The first-tier source market mainly includes seven relatively developed provinces/municipalities (Beijing, Tianjin, Shanghai, Guangdong, Fujian, Jiangsu, and Zhejiang) located in the eastern coastal areas of China, which contribute to roughly 50% of middle-class and well-off families of China. It owns 1,055 travel agencies engaged in outbound tourism, taking up 46% of the national total number. And the outbound tourist flow of these agencies accounts for 66% of the national total flow. The second-tier source market mainly includes 17 provinces/autonomous regions/municipalities (Heilongjiang, Jilin, Liaoning, Inner Mongolia, Shaanxi, Hebei, Shandong, Henan, Anhui, Shanxi, Hubei, Hunan, Jiangxi, Guangxi, Chongqing, Sichuan, and Hainan) in Central China, where 40% of middle-class and well-off families of China live and the GDP per capita of cities' and towns' population exceeds 5,000 U.S. dollars. It owns 1,089 travel agencies engaged in outbound tourism, taking up 47% of the national total number. And the outbound tourist flow of these agencies accounts for 32% of the national total flow. The third-tier source market mainly includes seven provinces/autonomous regions (Ningxia, Xinjiang, Qinghai, Gansu, Yunnan, Guizhou, and Tibet) in Southwest and Northwest China, which cover less than 10% of middle-class and well-off families, with relatively low GDP per capita of cities' and towns' population. It owns 165 travel agencies engaged in outbound tourism, taking up 7% of the national total number. And the outbound tourist flow of these agencies accounts for 3% of the national total flow.

In terms of features of market development, currently China's outbound tourism market is at the new stage of transformation and upgrading, presenting the following characteristics and trends: (1) outbound tourist flow continues to increase, and the second-tier source regions have great potential for growth; (2) tourist demand is diversified, personalized, and fragmented, with increasing demand for customized outbound tourism; (3) business positioning of outbound tourism operators and overseas suppliers starts to segment, and high-quality suppliers attract much more buyers and tourists; (4) consumption of China's outbound tourists continues to grow, but tending to be more rational; (5) FIT market develops fast, and will extend from neighboring destinations to long-haul destinations; (6) OTA (Online Travel Agent) is booming, and there are diversified types of operation in market.

The Tourism Law and Authentication and Evaluation Standard of High-Quality Service Suppliers of Outbound Tourism released last year will also promote transformation and upgrading of outbound tourism market. Despite nowadays outbound market is still faced with some challenges. This market has begun to segment, and quality tourism products are becoming more and more popular. China Association Of Travel Services (CATS) uses questionnaire to survey quarterly 50 to 100 key outbound travel agencies throughout the country. The latest survey shows that, 74%-93% of surveyed travel agencies are willing to cooperate with overseas high-quality suppliers. During questionnaire on outbound tourism market of 2015, CATS has optimistic expectations overall: 80% of travel agencies forecast Asian market will continue to grow; 82% forecast European market will continue to grow; 50% forecast American market will continue to grow, while 40% forecast the development of American market in 2015 will be similar to that in 2014; 56% forecast Oceanian market will continue to grow; 49% forecast African market will continue to grow, 41% forecast the development of African market in 2015 will be similar to that in 2014, and 10% forecast African market will drop.

By comprehensive evaluation on all factors of outbound tourism market, including macro-economy, airline capacity, visa policies of countries, and powerful promotion by tourism administrations of destinations, we anticipate that: in 2015 outbound tourism market will grow by 10% to 15% overall.

Since we don't have much time, the analysis of China's outbound tourism market has to come to an end. We, as a consulting company specializing in research on outbound tourism market, hope to communicate with you more in the future. Thank you!

Moderator:

Thank you, Dr. WANG! We just heard two comprehensive analysis reports. Next, the third speaker will discuss China's outbound tourism in several regions. Let's welcome my colleague, Mr. Amr Ghaffar, Regional director for the Middle East UNWTO. His speech is themed by The Middle East and North Africa Open the Door for Chinese Tourists.

Mr. Amr Ghaffar, the floor is yours!

The Middle East and North Africa Open the Door for Chinese Tourists

Mr. Amr Ghaffar (Regional director for the Middle East UNWTO)

(November 14, 2014, Shanghai, P. R. China)

Good afternoon, ladies and gentlemen,

It's indeed a great pleasure to be here with you and take part in this CITM thanks to CNTA and all the organizers for giving me this opportunity to share with you some information and thoughts on development trends and opportunity for tourism between China and MENA.

In my presentation, I shall be going essentially on with the study Chinese outbound travel to the Middle east and North Africa regions with the valuable technique support of Ivy alliance tourism consulting group.

I'm also going upon a series of market reports, national reports published quarterly that is called the tourism barometer, and lastly our forecasting study which is called tourism towards 2030, all these publications are available on UNWTO E-library.

Middle East and North Africa which comprises some 18 Arabic speaking countries, geographically between the Atlantic ocean and the Indian ocean, from Morocco West to South of Oman and the United Arab Emirates East. Both are unique varieties of attractions and resources that you have listed on the cover of this chart, which with strong interest and support of the government, and the initiative of the private sector, has particularly during the last decade, translated into a broad of core products that according to our research are very appealing to Chinese travelers, this product fit is likely to intensify in the coming decade.

Let me review the main characteristics of tourism in the Middle East and North Africa region with a series of facts and figures as you can see in this chart. The Middle East and North Africa is a region which has been growing very rapidly particularly during the last decade, recording growth rate of 11%, which is practically double the world's average, I'm taking the year 2010, in the beginning of 2011, the geopolitical environment in the region impacted negatively this rapid growth and stopped somehow, especially in the Middle East region, although this is a general trend, the picture is very risky because the situation is far from being homogeneous, whereas some traditional destinations are negatively affected, others in the gulf area continue to grow even at more rapid pace.

As you can see lower in the chart, corresponding to north Africa, the industry shows its resilience to external factors on many attentions, that you can see North Africa is recovering its positive growth pace, whereas the Middle East is growing more rapidly, but the trend is more dented because of the impact on the industry, it sustained to lose market share, but indicators that we have in UNWTO that probably by the end of this year, the curve is going to be again positive.

Now let's look at the main characteristics of Chinese travel to MENA region. The first remarks to make is that the growth of Chinese travel to the MENA region has been constant and very significant. in less than 15 years, it has grown from mere 50 000 tourist a year for year 2000, to more than five million recorded last year, only one destination in the region is the Emirates of Dubai accounts for more than half arrivals from China. Egypt, which was the traditional destination in the region for the Chinese tourism, down from its peak levels of 2010, but it's recovering previous level of visitation from Chinese tourists. There is strong interest in the history, civilization and unique heritage of the region on the one hand, and also that interest is supplemented by the attraction of the modern metropolis facilities and services, particularly in the golf area, such as Dubai, Doha and Abu Dhabi.

There is a significant shift as some of my previous speakers indicated from the standard group tours to more customized products and services, and also the increase tourist flow between China and MENA has positive impact on the development of business tourism, particularly on MICE.

There are also in our study a series of factors that are constraining the development of tourism from China to the region, they are listed in this chart. First is the geopolitical environment and safety-security perception by Chinese tourists. There is also need to improve the information about destinations and product offerings. There is insufficient or inconvenient air services, while Air Emirates greatly facilitates the tourist flow from China to Dubai and to other parts of the region. There is a lack of appropriate services as I mentioned. There is need to broaden the choices of tour programmes away from the standardized and insufficiently adapted to the preferences of different target groups of China, and finally there is lack of targeted promotions, obviously it should boost promotion and campaigns.

In terms of future prospects, our study concludes that prospects in medium even short term (over next 5 years) are Bullish; Dubai and Egypt will continue to be main destinations in the region; there is a number of emerging destinations will also enter Chinese market, such as Morocco, Tunisia and South Africa, and also Jordan and Middle East. There is also am increase that is expected in business and official travel which will grow significantly, particularly to the golf area.

Finally, our study provides some strategic guidelines on how to increase tourist flow from China to the region. Its three-level marketing strategies depending the maturity of the destination-for established, emerging and unknown destinations. Such as awareness raising, product development and differentiation. Quality improvements, cooperation with Chinese tour operators, establish presence in China. Participate in fairs and exhibitions like this symposium and improve air connectivity. We UNWTO are ready to promote and facilitate this partnership, public-public, public-private partnership between China and MENA to seize the rapidly changing opportunity from the market between both regions.

Thank you for your attentions!

Moderator:

Many thanks, Amr, for your excellent presentation. From the angle of MENA, for those who are not very familiar with this short term, MENA which means the Middle East and North Africa. But I would like to, before I pass on to next speaker, I want to do a little bit of promotion about MENA. Because I really like the key message that you just put it there. He says: the region has it all. You are not to do the promotion in the Chinese context, I want to switch to my Chinese language.

My colleague, Mr. Amr Ghaffar, Regional director for the Middle East, just introduced the Middle East and North Africa, which are unknown to most Chinese tourists. In his PPT, I noticed a word "the region has it all". Indeed, the region is little-known, but from point of view of tourist destination, it is a region full of pearls. The first choice or last choice of most Chinese travelers to Middle East is Dubai, while Mesopotamia, Abu Dhabi (also belonging to United Arab Emirates), Jordan, Amman, and Egypt are the untapped destinations for the Chinese. So I want to do a little bit of promotion here.

Next speaker is Mr. Adam Ruszinka, Deputy State Secretary for Tourism of Hungary. The title of his presentation is called The Tourism Cooperation between China and Central/Eastern Europe. Adam, the floor is yours!

The Tourism Cooperation between China and Central/Eastern Europe

Mr. Adam Ruszinka (Deputy State Secretary for Tourism of Hungary)

(November 14, 2014, Shanghai, P. R. China)

Dajia Xiawu hao! Good afternoon!

You know we have a very good representative here in China, so I'm learning Chinese very quickly.

Ladies and gentlemen,

Thank you very much for your invitation, and for this opportunity to give you a short presentation about tourism cooperation between China and Central and Eastern European countries.

Let me review with a few words to introduce the history of the Cooperation, There was an economic and Trade Forum of the 16 CEECs and China in Warsaw, April 2012, on this occasion, the Chinese prime minister advised to establish China-CEECs Association of Tourism Promotion Agencies and Businesses. This cooperation should be nice partnership to China. There are 16 topics in the Tourism Coordination Centre like agriculture, transportation, logistics, education, one of the important topics is of course tourism. And we Hungary are fortunate enough to be the leader of the cooperation. In May 2014, the first cooperation platform, in the field of tourism, was established.

How do we realize the cooperation? There are 16 Participating countries in Tourism Coordination Centre (TCC) set up in Budapest, in May 2014: Albania, Bosnia & Herzegovina, Bulgaria, Croatia, Czech Republic, Estonia, Hungary, Latvia, Lithuania, Macedonia, Montenegro, Poland, Romania, Serbia, Slovakia, Slovenia. The Operational costs are borne by Hungarian government, but we are only Committed to giving equal weight to participating countries.

What are the opportunities and benefits of the cooperation? China and Central and Eastern European countries have long-established relations in politics, economy and culture. China is a dynamically increasing long-haul source market for Central and Eastern Europe. Tourism platform may offer opportunities for CEE and China to adapt their tourism products to the needs of different cultures, help knowledge transfer, boost incoming tourism, develop air traffic routes and launch new flights. Another 5 cooperation platforms were established to further strengthen ties between China and CEE in various fields.

What's our mission and vision? Central and Eastern European countries shall promote and sell themselves as a single destination on the Chinese travel market. Joint promotion shall bring about the development of new tourism products, special and niche services, thus better satisfy the needs of the Chinese travellers to the CEE region. In the next ten years, the Central European region's share of Chinese outbound trips is expected to increase more than fivefold.

Here are some figures on Arrivals from China to Europe:

In 2013, 7.5 million Chinese tourists in Europe

Increasing average length of stay

In 2013, the CEE region received the most Chinese tourists after the Western European countries

This means 2.5 million tourists (33.5% of the travellers to Europe)

By 2018, the CEECs will receive 3.7 million (+46.4%) Chinese tourists

What are our key objectives? We need to deepen tourism cooperation between the CEECs and China, involve market players, increase the number of Chinese travellers and guest nights, reduce spatial concentration of tourist arrivals in Europe, provide reliable information for Chinese travellers, reach younger FIT travellers, share best practice, do experience-based joint marketing activity.

What are the main marketing tasks? We have to develop, coordinate and promote the relations between CNTA and the NTAs of the 16 CEECs, create and exchange databases containing the list of tourism industry players of China and the CEECs, contribute to the development of new tourism routes, products and packages, provide information for tourism industry players of the cooperating partners on visa related issues for tourism purposes, hold one forum per year with the aim of overviewing progress made and planning future activities, contribute to closer cooperation between national associations or enterprises of the tourism industry, Launch direct flights to the Central and Eastern European region from China, this is a very important issue indeed.

We have implemented some activities in 2014, such as contacting the 16 CEE countries, gathering country information for the common website content, preparing an e-statistical publication on 2013 data (a base for comparison in the development of tourism traffic between China and CEEC in the future), joint participation in China's International Travel Mart' 14 to 16 November, links referring to official tourism sites of CEE countries, placed on CNTA website, sharing press release and photos of the "Silk Road Project" for information and on-line publication on goals and activities of TCC in Chinese and English.

Here is the Planned Activities 2015:

A China Information Day Conference for international professional audience in Budapest

2nd Annual High-Level Meeting in one of the participating countries

On-line statistical publication on tourism data of 2014

A Pocket Guide' – mobile application for the general public presenting one tourism attraction per country,improving press relations, joint participation in CITM 2015, exhibition catalogue on Chinese and CEE tourism fairs and exhibition, education/knowledge transfer in the field of tourism between universities.

Thank you very much for your time and attention! Xiexie!

Moderator:

Thank you very much, Adam! I very much like one point you mentioned. At the beginning of your presentation, you said CNTA is an excellent partner, and I do share the same opinion with you that CNTA indeed is also an excellent partner with UNWTO. Thank you, advisement you do, and also for your patience to be here throughout with us. Probably you want to look at this particular presentation made by Adam. From the angle that to penetrate the Chinese market. It's not just about promotion for the sake of promotion. It is also about establishing an institution, making your promotion of Chinese market as a source market institutionalized. And this is the center that is established by our friends in Central and East Europe countries together with the Chinese partner, where the promotion has been conducted with evidence based research. This is where the key probably lies for the previous presentation. The other thing that I want to share with you, ladies and gentleman, is that you might have known is that we choose this presenter. We didn't choose from the mature destinations such as France, or Germany, or England, but we choose relatively lower awared destinations of Europe, relating to Eastern Europe countries. Thank you once again, Adam, for your excellent and thought-breaking presentation. Now, our next speaker, who is the last speaker for our session, is my good and old friend,

Ms. Sonja Hunter, who held the Samoa tourism authority as its CEO but also more importantly, Sonja is also the chairperson of South Pacific Tourism Organization. This is another, if you judge from the title of her presentation, is called "South Pacific Islands: the Next Destination", is the same thing why we choose this area, because this area is the untapped destinations for the Chinese. Sonja, the floor is yours.

South Pacific Islands—The Next Destinations

Ms. Sonja Hunter (Chief executive officer of Samoa tourism Authority)

(November 14, 2014, Shanghai, P. R. China)

I'd like to take this opportunity to thank CNTA, UNWTO for allowing me to present South Pacific here in this symposium. Yes, it's very good to have good partnership with CNTA, and CNTA has a seat in South pacific tourism director board. Before I start, I'd like to give a snapshot about the south pacific tourism organization, it comprises 16 member countries, including china, our office locates Fiji.

Tourism in the Pacific Region ~ IT IS ALL ABOUT YOU~ we want to engage our tourists as much as possible, be able to understand them, be able to see what they like, be able to develop the wonderful relationship so to improve the customer loyalty and partnerships.

Ladies and gentlemen, I'd like to tell you a little bit about how big our region is. When it comes to south pacific, people usually say, oh, that's a bunch of little islands which don't have any natural resources, but ladies and gentlemen, we are the next destination, the new destination, why? 150 million Indians on 50 million sqkm. We are definitely growing, and surely you will enjoy it.

I want you to know something about our region, look at the pictures, we have miles of miles of coasts, aside from marine activities like diving. We also inspire people with a lot of different products, such as bungee jumping, and so on. Our culture is also full of different music and dancing. Most people enjoy the authentic fire dance for example, some other cultures like to walk on fire, if you see it, please don't do it at home. Apart from the original culture, I want give you a few snapshots on what's available on pacific. The different hotels and lodgings can meet different needs of clients. With 50 million sqkm, we have very fresh and delicious food as well, you have your cuisine, we have ours. We try our best to keep its freshness. At the end of the day, we are doing this for reasons. We enjoy and we understand each other, you understand our culture and everybody around the world is able to enjoy, because that's what holiday is all about. It's not about going away or about money, but it's about understanding the places that you visit like we do today. We visit China. We enjoy Chinese cuisine. Some people say you don't say something about the branding, I think it is true, once we know what the Chinese like or dislike, we have different adaptation set at home, so that's why we say in pacific, tourism it's all about the clients, it's all about you. We have fashion show. We are also able to provide perfectly romantic wedding to our clients. We also would like to say that we are not in the way to live in cities. We have all the comforts and different technologies you have. For instance, we have multi Media and Telecommunication Capabilities. You know the young Chinese market request wifi service anywhere they visit with smart phones. Some others are quite challenging. We have built efficient electricity progressing towards renewable energy capabilities, looking to quality water supply, access connectivity to major source markets: airlines and cruise ships. You many take it for grounded, but for us it was some efforts done. These are challenges, but also a lot of opportunities, but we enjoyed it, why? Because in the pacific region, we look after everyone, we promote safety, healthy and friendly environment, we can't live without educated workforces in all areas crucial to tourism as well, because they are the ones to tell stories, and they are the ones who are going to serve everything to everyone that comes to our region.

Why do people visit us? People are warm and friendly. pristine and relaxing with fresh food, interesting culture and unique activities, warm and summer all year, law and order with no armaments/guns, handicraft, art, fashion, designer goods, other games, sports, corporate and adventures that entertains and provides meaningful experiences and lasting memories.

We are definitely growing, the average annual growth rate of Chinese visitors to the Pacific for the last 5 years (2009-2013) is 46.4 percent. Increase in regional numbers led by Fiji.

At last but not the least, can we play the video? Only 60 seconds?

Enjoy and Thank you very much!

Moderator:

Thank you, Sonja. Thank you very much. Friend or not friend, life is tough for moderator. But still let's give a round of applause to Sonja.

With that, I'll like you to give a big hand to all the speakers and I am now pass the floor to the next session, for the panel discussion to Dr. WANG Xinjun.

Panel Discussion 2　China Outbound Tourism in Transformation-Opportunities, Potential and Challenges

Moderated by Mr. WANG Xinjun, CEO of IVY Alliance Tourism Consulting

(November 14, 2014, Shanghai, China)

Moderator:

Good afternoon! I am very glad to host the panel discussion on outbound tourism. In this session we invite six heavyweight guests, who come from a Chinese outbound travel agency, an airline, three destination countries, and a regional international organization.

Let's welcome them, they are:

Mr. ZHANG Shigang, Vice President of China Travel Services

Mr. HE Zhigang, Managing Director, Marketing Department, Air China Ltd.

Mr. David Craig, General Manager Asia, Tourism New Zealand

Mr. Riccardo Strano, Director Asia – Oceania, ENIT-Italian Government Tourist Board in China

Mr. WU Dawei, Tourism Officer, ASEAN China Centre

Mr. Abualmaaty Shaarawy, Tourism Counselor, the Egyptian Embassy in China

Please take a seat, each speaker.

Thanks for your participation in today's panel discussion, to contribute your opinions to China's outbound tourism market. I will ask six speakers different questions.

I'd like to ask Mr. ZHANG, Vice President of China Travel Services, the first question. China's outbound tourism has developed for many years, does the current outbound market present some new changes or characteristics?

Emerging Changes and Characteristics of China Outbound Tourism Market

Mr. ZHANG Shigang (Vice President of China Travel Services)

(November 14, 2014, Shanghai, P. R. China)

Thank you, moderator!

I am ZHANG Shigang, Vice President of China Travel Services.

I want to briefly answer the question in several aspects. Firstly, China's outbound tourism has changed from luxury consumption in the past to mass demand. Secondly, besides travel agencies and tourism enterprises, other industries like banking, finance, sport, and culture have taken part in the tourism industry. Thirdly, outbound tourism products have developed from long-haul tour in several counties within over 10 days to short-distance tour in a single country or in-depth tour in one or two countries, and outbound tourism is becoming shorter and more economical. In the past, we might travel to foreign countries once a year or two, but now we want to go abroad each quarter, or for all holidays, which makes Asian countries near China much hotter. Moreover, in the past group tours were main stream of outbound travel, but nowadays FIT travelers segments are growing fast, and there are diversified types of FIT tours, extending from past "plane ticket + hotel" service to self-driving, island holidaying, and so on, these ways are changing constantly. That's all. Thank you!

Moderator:

Many thanks, Vice President ZHANG, for your share. At present, more than 2,300 Chinese travel agencies are engaged in outbound tourism, each travel agency has its own market positioning or operation mode. So, Mr. ZHANG, can you tell us what measures has China Travel Services (CTS) taken to improve operation mode of outbound tourism and guarantee quality of service? Please give us a snapshot about this.

ZHANG Shigang:

As everyone knows, China Travel Services (CTS) is the first travel agency in China, as well as an affiliate of China National Travel Service (HK) Group Corporation, which is the largest travel group in China. CTS commits itself to providing the public with first-class service, high-quality reception, and reasonable price. Firstly, as a travel agency with a long history, CTS opposes low-price competition, and believes that only when we refuse to meet distorted demand of market by low price can we assure tourists receive due quality of service, and regulate market order. Secondly, CTS always advocates and supports the Tourism Law released in 2014, constantly contributing to standardization of tourism product, improvement of service quality, guidance and normalization of civilized travel of outbound tourists, etc. Thirdly, besides having a long history, CTS owns an enormous travel agency network, 128 branches at home and abroad. Meanwhile, CTS has its own e-commerce platform—Mancocity.com. All these resources ensure we are able to continuously satisfy requirements of tourists from all walks of life. In addition, we make our travel agency network, e-commerce network, products, and sales channels open to all enterprises in the tourism industry and all markets in society. We don't grow independently, but together with you. That's all. Thank you!

Moderator:

Many thanks, Mr. ZHANG, for your share and description!

Moderator:

We know, airline is an important component of outbound tourism market, then, I'd like to ask Managing Director HE from Air China: from airline point of view, what do you think of the development potential of China's outbound tourism market? Does Air China have any plan for air route and transport capacity next year or in the next two years, to increase any new destination route? Let's welcome Mr. HE to present some information to us.

Adapting to the Transformation of China Outbound Tourism Market with Better Airline Services

Mr. HE Zhigang (Managing Director, Marketing Department, Air China Ltd.)

(November 14, 2014, Shanghai, P. R. China)

With regard to China's outbound tourism, I believe Vice Chairman DU Jiang, President DAI Bin, and you certainly have correcter forecast than us. Of course, Air China also always pays much attention to the development of China's tourism, especially of outbound tourism. A moment ago Mr. ZHANG described characteristics of China's outbound tourism, so I won't give unnecessary details. With regard to number of planes, by 2015 Air China will possess 82 wide-bodies planes, which are able to fly for over eight hours. Therefore we have enough transport capacity to fly to all places in the world. Air China constantly explores in the international field, for example, some time ago when German Chancellor visited China, Air China and Lufthansa reached a consensus on further cooperation; when Canadian Prime Minister visited China during APEC, Air China and Air Canada reached a consensus on further cooperation as well. Within China, Air China owns first-tier, second-tier, and third-tier airports. Maybe your impression is that Air China only offers international flight service, but actually we are a big family, having family members like Shenzhen Airlines, Shandong Air, Air Macau, Dalian Airlines, Tibet Airlines, and Inner Mongolia Airlines, basically covering all inlands and major cities of China. After two-year's integration, Air China is playing an enormous role, and nowadays on the strength of

Air China network people can enter and leave China freely and conveniently. Thanks to the policy of 72-hour transit visa exemption in several cities, inbound tourism has grown stably. I believe, along with the in-depth application of relevant policies, inbound tourism will develop faster and faster. In outbound tourism respect, former speakers mentioned many beautiful destinations like long-history Middle East and some islands, to which we also pay great attention. In the near future, Air China will open new air routes to countries along One Belt One Road, and new air routes to link China and Africa/the Caribbean Sea region as well. Thank you!

Moderator:

Many thanks, Mr. HE, for your presentation! I still have another question: China's inbound tourism market is in process of transformation, FIT travelers are increasing, in this regard, does Air China offer any new product to this group of people? Or, does Air China cooperate with travel agencies and tourism administrations of destinations on this market? Can you tell us something about this?

HE Zhigang:

Thank you! Over the past two years Air China has made great attempts, constantly cooperating with overseas travel agencies and introducing foreign destinations to Chinese people. For instance, in 2014 Air China launched air routes to Hawaii and Washington, and we have conducted fine cooperation with state tourism administrations of the two states and with GoUSA. Certainly, we also have cooperated with offices of CNTA in other countries, such as promoting "beautiful China" launched by CNTA. We hope to establish a platform, to provide domestic travel agencies more opportunities to show themselves in foreign countries. In the light of features of current outbound tourism, Air China has improved type of airplane and passenger product to a large extent. In the newly introduced airplane 747-8, we set four types of seat: first class and business class for public affairs, and super-economy class and economy class. The super-economy class is very suitable for the foregoing "two rich and one middle-class" (rich family, rich single, and middle-class family) group. It isn't so expensive, but very comfortable. For more information, I am willing to share with you afterwards. Thank you!

Moderator:

Thank you, Mr. HE!

Moderator:

I'd like to ask Mr. David Craig next question. More and more Chinese are going to New Zealand, and in 2014 the tourist flow will reach roughly 300, 000. As a promotion officer of Tourism New Zealand in Asian market, especially in Chinese market, what do you think of the differences between current and past China-New Zealand tourism products? Just now Mr. ZHANG gave his opinions from point of view of travel agency. As a representative from destination's tourism administration, what do you think of the development of such market?

Upgrading of New Zealand Tourist Products & Quality Service to Chinese Tourists

Mr. David Craig (General Manager Asia, Tourism New Zealand)

(November 14, 2014, Shanghai, P. R. China)

Xiawu hao! (Hello)

Yes, you are right, the Chinese market is very important, we've got a quarter of million Chinese visitors every year, FIT travelers segments are growing about 60% this year, of course, we still a lot of group tours. That reflects the changing of Chinese tastes. We see the Chinese want to take part. They want to try things rather than in the past generally reserved in sightseeing. We saw Sonja introduced bungee jumping in pacific. There are plenty of Chinese bungee jumping, and doing some softer activities as well. I think, not long ago, they would tend to go to tourist spots such as Queensland, now they are traveling widely across the country even some less known places. They stay longer, so the average stay was quite low, now it increased about 30%. They explore the country, starting to try self-driving, new accommodation, that actually puts us in quite a challenge for new design tailored for Chinese tourists.

For us we are trying to build a sustainable relationship, we certainly try to carry the shift to quality services. We know that the biggest driver of the destination choice is words of mouth. If Chinese have good travel experience in New Zealand, then that will lead to more Chinese visitation. What we do to promote the country of is to have communication with opinion leaders so that they can tell their version of the story. A

couple of years ago, some of you might know, we invited Yaochen, and she liked the country so much. She decided to get married there, which created a nice cycle for us. And this year, we cooperated with Hunan TV on babaqunar (Daddy, where are we going) the first international film showed celebrities and children actually doing things. We want to show that New Zealand is not only a beautiful place, but also an interesting place where there are many things you can do. That show has given us a huge rage into the Chinese market. It's also delivering the strategy that is to bring New Zealand to life for Chinese families. So target for 2015 is to continue the communicate as we did.

Moderator:

Many thanks, Mr. David Craig, for your description and share!

Moderator:

This year is the 10th anniversary of the time EU countries became China's outbound tourism destination. Europe is always a desirable long-haul destination for Chinese tourists, and Italia is a typical sub-destination. I'd like to ask Mr. Riccardo Strano: you are a tourism marketing expert with rich experience, and you also have worked in different countries on behalf of Italian Government Tourist Board. From your point of view, what are the differences between Chinese market and other source markets? What is your opinion?

Characteristics of China Outbound Tourism Market & Italian Interpretation

Mr. Riccardo Strano (Director Asia – Oceania, ENIT-Italian Government Tourist Board in China)

(November 14, 2014, Shanghai, P. R. China)

Thank you very much for having me here, thank you for the great job you did. So there is no doubt that everybody is following Chinese tourists. For our side, Italy is one of the point of European destinations, so Chinese now travel to Europe. Italy is like a stop-over, like a short visit, they want to do much more, but they don't have time, so that's why we are following the FIT. Maybe you want to try to change the meaning in tourism and travel, we want to change the possibility into a qualified destination. That means we have to work very hard. In our country, for instance, I want to criticize my position, it's that we have a vision, visa problems to be solved. Secondly, some people say that in China people don't speak English. This is an initiative, and we have to work on that. That the reason why you are a huge market coming, we have to be very careful. We have to work with much more attention that we man manage. At the same time, we have to work on our products. Italy could be the main door to Europe. we are very much aware of our position. We are going very well, because when Chinese decide to travel to Europe, they decide to travel to Italy, I saw some date it showed they are very satisfied. But we have to work very much. We want to match the different desire and wishes of the tourists. Second, we should encourage our entrepreneurs to cooperate with Chinese tour operators. Although everyone take Chinese tourists as big shopper, we want to be secure. If you have chance to make shopping, you have to select very seriously following the quality. That's because you don't have to waste your money and your time. You have to keep a beautiful memory when you pack for your travel. I hope Italy is a good memory for you. When you return, you will have to make your experience again, it will be much deeper. That's where we talk about niche products. For me, you are the most important market, we have to be very serious, and careful.

We will have the most important event next year. It is Expo Milan 2015, like Shanghai years ago. We expect a lot of Chinese tourists since you have 3 pavilions. We want to reinforce the capacity to be much more informed about different opportunities about Italy. Italy is very well-known because it's a cultural country, full of art, food and wine and shopping. I don't want my country just to be a shopping destination. We have wide range of products. I do think shopping is very important, but if you try to be more graduated in tourism, you have an opportunity to grow your knowledge about the world.

Moderator:

Thank you, Mr. Riccardo Strano! We also hope much more Chinese tourists will visit Expo Milan 2015 next year.

Moderator:

I want to ask Mr. WU Dawei, who is from ASEAN China Centre, next question. ASEAN Countries are the earliest destinations for China's outbound tourism, and now receive the most Chinese tourists. From your point of view, after years' development, what potential can we still seek in China's outbound market? Moreover, what challenges does this market face? What is your opinion of these?

Huge Potential & Challenges ASEAN Attracting Chinese Tourists

Mr. WU Dawei (Tourism Officer, ASEAN China Centre)

(November 14, 2014, Shanghai, P. R. China)

Ok, thank you, moderator! With regard to potential, we can say that ASEAN Countries have huge potential. We can see "huge potential" from two aspects, the first is hardware environment: ASEAN Countries are close to China, so tourists can enjoy relatively shorter air range, with moderate price. Secondly, the climate of ASEAN Countries is mild in general, suitable for traveling all the year around, which is very attractive to Chinese tourists, especially to those in North China. From the perspective of tourist resources, ASEAN Countries are abundant in natural and cultural tourist resources, owning numerous islands and beaches, as well as world cultural and historic heritage. These resources have huge potential, with high price/performance ratio.

Of course, from another angle, ASEAN Countries still have much work to do. Do you have any question in this regard?

Moderator:

What challenges does this market face? From your point of view, what improvements can ASEAN Countries conduct upon structure of tourism product, quality of service, and transformation of product?

WU Dawei:

I want to answer this question from two aspects. Firstly, advertisement and sales promotion of tourism. Chinese tourists are familiar with classic ASEAN tourism products like "Singapore-Malaysia-Thailand". For a long period of time, "Singapore-Malaysia-Thailand" had been a stepping-stone to outbound tourism, and on the basis of this, Chinese tourists went farther and farther. Other similar products like Vietnam-Cambodia are becoming mature gradually. Moreover, thanks to the open sky policy signed jointly by China and ASEAN in 2011, the development and expansion of bilateral civil air routes has crossed the barriers of policy and technology. We are much delighted at seeing that, at the end of 2013, Air China opened flight course from Beijing to Cambodia, and now we also have regular direct flight from Beijing to Chiang Mai, Thailand. All these highly drive development of new products and growth of tourist flow.

Moderator:

Many thanks, Mr. WU, for your presentation!

We also notice that, nowadays more and more Chinese tourists begin to travel to Africa and Middle East, and previously Regional director for the Middle East UNWTO also told us something about these regions. Egypt is a key destination for Chinese tourists. I want to ask Dr. Abualmaaty: what is the position of Chinese market in Egyptian international tourism market? In addition, through years' development, especially since this year, we find there are changes in ways of traveling and route selection of Chinese tourists to Egypt, can you, from point of view of Egypt Tourism, give us some presentation?

Egyptian Unique Tourist Products & Tailor-Made Services to Attract Chinese Outbound Tourists

Dr. Abualmaaty Shaarawy (Tourism Counselor, the Egyptian Embassy in China)

(November 14, 2014, Shanghai, P. R. China)

First of all, I'd like to thank CNTA and UNWTO for inviting us to participate this forum and discuss with you about Chinese outbound tourism and other aspects.

Dajia Xiawuhao! As you know, China's outbound tourism market is growing rapidly, according to the last presentation here from China Tourism Academy, outbound tourists will reach over 110 million in 2014, making China No.1 outbound source market in the world. Egypt is a perfect destination for its unique ancient civilization that Chinese tourists prefer to other competitors. So we market Egypt as a country with culture, heritage and civilization. There were 110,000 Chinese tourists visited Middle East, among which over 65,000 Chinese tourists went to Egypt in 2013, it makes Egypt No.1 destination in Middle East.

We are promoting Egypt through our offices in Beijing, Shanghai and Guangzhou. We are also making efforts to create more promotion centers in the second and third tier cities like Tianjin, Qingdao, Dalian, in this way, our goal is to have more and more market share of Chinese outbound travel.

Nowadays, the capital city Cairo became the hub to Africa and Middle East. Transportation network is well done, connecting South Africa, Dubai, Jordon etc. We look forward to receiving more and more Chinese tourists in the near future, of course, we will do as much as we can to provide better facilitation in visa policy, tourist service, and infrastructure.

Thank you!

Moderator:

Many thanks, Dr. Abualmaaty, for your description! That's all for today's panel discussion on outbound tourism. Many thanks go to the six speakers, thank you very much!